THE HULL & SCARBOROUGH RAILWAY

By
C.T. Goode

Front Cover:
D49 No. 62769 'The Oakley' waits beneath the roof of Bridlington station, with a service to Scarborough. *Photo. C T Goode*

Back Cover: "Come to sunny Bridlington", a railway poster typical of the thirties, courtesy of Crewe North Railway Museum, and a couple of old railway tickets.

ISBN 1 870313 21 6
72 Woodland Drive Anlaby,Hull HU10 7HX

Printed by: Burstwick Print & Publicity Services,
13a Anlaby Road, Hull. HU1 2PJ

Contents

Foreword.

This book is the last of a series which has encompassed the railways of Yorkshire from Sheffield to Wakefield, Leeds, York and Scarborough, with runs down to Selby and Goole. They are all in the same format and,I hope, up (or down) to the same standard. It is a little strange, perhaps, for one to have left this work until last, as I travelled to work with its help for nine years and met some good railway friends on my travels. Mr. Bedale was a Relief Stationmaster who was keen to learn foreign languages while travelling to work, and Mr. Pearson, father of Jill, Stationmaster at Bridlington who bent the rules a little to allow me entry to the often beautifully kept booking offices at some of the closed stations. In those days permanent way gangs travelled by the appropriate trains, up to ten at a time and were often dropped off specially, wherever they were working, a lively lot.

My thanks as always to the staff of local studies libraries at Beverley, Hull and Bridlington; also to Ann of the K. Hoole Library at Darlington North Road.

C. Tony Goode.

Anlaby, Hull.

May 2000.

EARLY DAYS IN HULL AND BRIDLINGTON

Hull has a long, and perhaps surprisingly for its situation, interesting history which really began around 1293 when King Edward the First obtained it from the monks of Meaux Abbey, who had been using it as their landing place up the river Hull. The king showed great interest in the place, which was expanding steadily, and visited there in April 1300. He crossed the Humber between Barton and Hessle, interrupting his journey north to visit the new borough, one which was thriving almost entirely on water borne trade. Soon, however, roads sprang up serving each possible direction and, though a journey was often lengthy, some sort of rapport came to be established between neighbours in York, Selby or Scarborough and beyond. At first Hull numbered about 2,000 but steadily increased, particularly due to the Industrial Revolution and the growth in the use of horse power and stage coaches.

By 1900 the population stood at around 238,600 and is indeed almost double that number today, containing in its streets every kind of interest and diversion that can be mentioned. The stage coaches of the 1780-1840 period served quite well to link up Hull with the outside world, and took in nicely the area covered by this little work. In 1833 the 'Express' was running between Hull and Scarborough and had connections north to Scotland. It left the Victoria Hotel at 6 am. and reached Scarborough at 12.15 pm. to go forward at 4 pm. The return trip also left Scarborough at 6 am., reaching Hull at midday, running to the Humber ferry where, after a crossing to Barton passengers could join a London service which would reach the capital at noon on the following day. At Bridlington the 'British Queen' left at 7 am., running via Brandesburton and reaching Hull at 11 am., with a return from Hull at 4 pm. to reach the 'Stirling Castle Hotel in Bridlington at 8 pm. Both named coaches belonged to the same company, one of two which operated the services.

None of the places served by the branch has much of the historical about it; Filey will be dealt with as we reach it, as will be Driffield. Bridlington has, however, some claim to the reader's attention, with antiquity in both the Old Town and Harbour which are some distance apart. The Old Town, some 1 1/2 miles away from the sea, has the Priory church which is 185ft. long by 78ft. wide, this being the nave of the original structure, as the dreaded Dissolution saw off the transepts with a central tower and the chancel, leaving a somewhat bleak remainder. Of especial interest is the west front which has two towers, that to the left stunted, that to the right (west) made much higher during the Victorian restoration of Giles Gilbert Scott by the addition of pinnacles. Originally the Priory was the home of Augustinian Canons, but like Whitby declined, due to the attention of marauding Scots and Danes. Its most famous Prior was John de Bridlington (1366-79) whose grave, behind the high altar, was allegedly a place of great miracles. Of more recent date an obelisk in the church reminds one of the 46 sailors who died in the storm of February 1871, representing 23 families.

Now, having mentioned the sea one is reminded of the fate of Henrietta Maria who landed here on her return from Holland in 1643, loaded with arms which had been exchanged for the crown jewels. Batten, the Parliamentary Admiral, pursued her, bombarding the town and driving the Queen to the shelter of a ditch. Once this passed, however, the lady came out of hiding and, still with her ammunition, stayed for a fortnight at a lodging house in Queen Square. The Old Town was little more than a village with a single high street of small shops. The Quay was different, well built with large properties stretching from where the station was to be to the seaside which now has promenades to the south and north of two piers, the longer one of which is used by anglers. Larger buildings included the Floral Pavilion with a floral clock of 1907, and a box-like Grand Pavilion of thirty years later. The best single reason for visiting the town is the superb view of the rake of cliffs to the north, topped by the old and new Flamborough lighthouses.

EARLY RAILWAYS

Hull was reached first of all by rail, which followed a largely straight and level run along the bank of the Humber from a junction with the Leeds & Selby Railway at the latter place. An Act was obtained for the line on 21st June 1836, with a working capital of £533,333 and the Engineer, Mr Walker, in charge. There were to be three water crossings, the first, that over the Ouse next to the station at Selby the trickiest to manage. Initially it was suggested that the route should divert to take in the Caves, North and South; probably with a desire, half anticipated, to pre-empt the later line of the Hull & Barnsley some fifty years later. Initially, too, the plan was for the line to enter Hull north of Hessle road and to end near to Mytongate bridge, so closer to the town than did in fact happen. In fact a continuation of the original straight line was

A View taken in the 1920s showing the dockland and its railways to the west of Hull. Prominent is the footbridge over the yards leading on from Strickland Street to the left, then, following upwards to the right, the later MS & L (Great Central) goods depot of the three bays alongside Kingston Street looking up Commercial Road. Beyond this, towards the centre is the NER Kingston Street engine shed and the vast NER goods depot of ten bays fronting Railway Street with the L & Y depot along side it. On this site was the old NER station. Photo: Hull Museums

projected eastwards along the river bank to English street by the Humber dock and a stone's throw from the ferry across the river. This line was opened on 1st July 1840.

Earlier than this, in 1833 a project had been mooted to send a line from the Quay at Bridlington to join the Leeds & Selby Railway in a similar manner; likewise, in the following year a committee at Bridlington voted in favour of a similar venture to reach York which would run by way of Driffield and Pocklington to reach the new line from York to Leeds, somewhat circuitous one might have thought. Both projects foundered after one look at the daunting heights of the Wolds, even though it was held that, once on the other side, the lines would for the most part be level. Vigorous promotion of the latter scheme stressed development of trade with the Baltic ports and that imports of fish could readily reach the West Riding, while the line would distribute agricultural and other bounty of the area, as follows:

Fish:	£22,000 p.a.
Driffield goods:	£6,000 p.a.
Coal and slates:	£2,500 p.a.

The passenger potential was probably more realistic at £2,000. The Report hoped for the development of lands around the Quay as 'Docks and other conveniences at a comparatively trifling expense'.

In many cases early railway schemes are held over in a given area until a much later date, as in this case when it was not until 1884 when the Scarborough-Bridlington & West Riding Jc. Railway was opened through the Wolds from Driffield to Market Weighton, a small but hilly part of an adventurous whole with an independent existence until 1914 when it was taken over by the NER. The line was very busy at weekends, running traffic on and off the sleeping branch from Market Weighton at Selby. Thus, the honour of those earlier Bridlington men of foresight was partially satisfied, but at a price.

Railway matters were not to be raised for a time until the subject was to be found in the midst of a welter of parliamentary authorisations during 1844-5 when a total of 247 new miles of railway were subsidised to the tune of £3 ½ million pounds. Here the Hull & Selby sought powers to construct a branch from Hull to Bridlington, giving estimated receipts for passengers carried of £15,898 and goods of £12,072, though it is always hard to see where such estimates could possibly come from. On 18th February 1845 the Bill had its first reading and was introduced by Lord Hotham, Sir John Hanmer and Sir Walter James, receiving the Royal Assent on 3rd June 1845. In the same session powers were given to the York & North Midland to run a line from Seamer, on the York-Scarborough line, to Bridlington, 19 3/4 miles; that to Hull being 31 miles. The section between Filey and Bridlington had the greatest number of curves and gradients, which delayed the opening of this part by thirteen days. Thus, the Bridlington-Filey section opened on 5th October 1846, the Hull line one day later and the Filey-Seamer portion on the 18th.

The Hull line was easy to build, under supervision of Mr J. C. Birkinshaw of York and contractors Jackson & Bean of Driffield. The steepest gradient was 1 in 177 for a short distance, the main bugbear being the level crossings, of which there were 37. Here it was a case of sacrificing goodwill from the lineside folk to cheapness in not having expensive bridges which would have needed costly run-ups on each side in all cases. There were already plans for a joint station in Bridlington, but the day was saved by George Hudson who took the two companies under his capacious wing. The architect was Mr G. T. Andrews, who was to produce good quality station buildings and houses, sturdily built, with most still in existence. Out of the platforms at Bridlington there is a continuous, nagging climb of five miles at 1 in 92 to near Speeton, part in cutting, part curved and with occasional fine views of the coastline. Thereafter the line falls more gently towards Seamer, though still sinuous.

THE OPENING DAY

For the opening of the parent line between Hull and Selby four engines were used: 'Kingston', 'Exley', 'Andrew Marvell' and 'Prince', together with four trains of 32 coaches. The first left at 12.15 pm. for Selby and took two hours en route, though the return journey with 'Prince' took only a little over the hour. In the goods warehouse at the Hull terminus the 760 guests found 15 tables loaded with a cold banquet. Afterwards there followed the usual run of speeches full of vain hopes and self-glorification in some cases, chaired by Henry Broadley MP, the star of the event being Alderman George Hudson, the great prime mover, who responded to the toast, including in his text mention of his other projects in Yorks. and Lancs. and offering words of thanks to his partner, George Stephenson.

Six years later, on Tuesday 8th October 1846 the branch line to Bridlington was opened, for which 11,000 tickets were issued. At first the weather was inclement and those in Hull had to wait for 3/4 hour until the train arrived carrying Hudson and the York directors. The twenty two coaches were attached to the 44 holding the eagerly waiting Hull contingent and quite quickly the train, drawn by three engines, 'Hudson', 'Antelope' and 'Aeriel', products of the Railway Foundry, Leeds, set off. Incidentally, these trains were never as long as they sounded, since the carriages of the time were little longer than wagons; still, 66 wagons would need three engines on anyone's railway!

By the time the train reached Cottingham the weather-god had relented, and the wet and dismal 'thirds' were cheered by the shining forth of the sun. In addition to the invited guests, there were two bands aboard to enliven the journey. It was recorded that numerous parties were assembled at the various stations on the line, and from Driffield to Bridlington the road was lined with people.

It was originally intended that the line between Beverley and Bridlington should be single, but before its construction was completed it had been doubled and the electric telegraph, which was then a novelty, was installed too.

While the train was making for Bridlington, feverish arrangements were being made to welcome it. Mr. Ingram said the locals had not been idle, and that at 9 am. a procession had begun to be formed at the Market Place. There were two bands.

It was estimated that 2,000 people met the train. It had taken about two hours to reach Bridlington, and as it had not left until 11.10 am. the Bridlington spectators must have been tired of waiting. Stops had been made at Cottingham, Beverley and Driffield, where several people had joined the party.

On arrival the directors and their guests proceeded to the goods station where luncheon was provided, there being between 1,400 and 1,600 sitting down. A Mr Rycroft of the 'Quay' provided the meal. George Hudson presided and had on his right and left the Lord and Lady Mayor and Mayoress of York. The Lord Mayor of Hull was present, this being the first time the first citizens of the two places had met in public. Mr Hudson proposed the toast 'prosperity' to the town and port of Bridlington and praised the enterprise of the English people, pointing out that, whereas in England at that time there were 4,000 miles of railway, in France there were only 400. He complimented the Bridlington people on the beauty of the town's situation.

A congratulatory address couched in flowing and rather hypocritical terms was presented to Mr. Hudson.

The main party returned to Hull at about 3.30 pm., the time between the luncheon and departure being spent walking about the village or on the Quay. Bridlington's celebrations concluded in the evening with a display of fireworks near the terminus, the first rocket being fired at 7 pm.

On the return journey the train reached Hull at 5 pm. A dinner had been arranged in the Assembly Rooms, but someone had apparently bungled the arrangements, for the guests were invited for 5 pm. and the doors were not open until 7 pm. The meal, however, compensated the guests for the delay. It was recorded that ‘for profusion, delicacy, style and quality it could scarcely be surpassed. The wines were particularly good, but though they seemed to have loosened the tongues, all was not harmony’.

When the line was first opened to the public, there were five trains each way daily, each taking about 2 hours’. (Bridlington Free Press: 12.10.1946)

Rates had already been fixed for passengers, namely 1st Class 3d. per mile, 2nd Class 2d. and 3rd Class 1 1/2d, the first listed having an allowance of up to 150 lb. free luggage, the rest 100 lb. Third class travellers would enjoy the double benefits from riding in the open carriages, smoke from the engine and losing their hats on the way. At first there were four trains each way on weekdays, and one on Sundays, First Return being 4/-, Second 3/- and Third 2/-. Tickets had to be booked on the day previously and there was one common return fare for the first excursion ever, that to Hull Fair, a week after the opening.

Some of the vehicles used in the portion which ran from the old station in Hull, to be replaced in 1848 by the new Paragon station, were of interesting construction; the ‘Tourist’, a glass roofed affair like a mobile conservatory, alongside the ‘Coquette’, like a doll’s house, beautifully made vehicles from a firm in Manchester. These elegant specimens jostled with the cast-offs, the humble open thirds which had no cover from rain and murk.

Stations on the way were at Cottingham, Beverley, Arram, Lockington, Hutton Cranswick and Driffield, Nafferton, Lowthorpe, Burton Agnes and Carnaby. As far as can be discovered, all these existed at the opening, the least likely being Arram and Carnaby, neither of which would be likely to attract much custom. All were in the G. T. Andrews style. Beyond Bridlington the style was often different, with stations at Flamborough (Marton at first), Bempton, Speeton, Hunmanby and Filey, followed by the make-weights of Gristhorpe and Cayton, before Seamer.

Our ancestors had three years to travel from Hull to Bridlington from the original station by Humber Dock, a building of white stone 100 ft. by 70 ft. with front offices and a passageway to the train shed, 'lit' by 22 windows complemented by the same number of columns. There were two platforms flanking four lines for the storage of rolling stock, each leading to three small turntables for manoeuvring the small vehicles, a popular idea at this time. The roadway was to the north of the site. The first trains were halted outside the station and drawn into the station by stationary engine, perhaps because the early drivers could not be trusted, or were unable to get the brakes on in time. Soon, however, engines would run to the rear of the trains and push them in.

THE LINE DESCRIBED - HULL TO BEVERLEY

The journey out was along the river bank westwards, with the three road engine shed on the left and the old House of Correction on the right, built for the general public and not purely for railway employees. As the early map of 1853 shows, this was a circular building, complete with treadmill. Once at Dairycoates Jc., later to be the site of vast railway activity and the site of one of the largest loco. depots, the line turned north to run straight up to a point later to be Cottingham South Jc. where it would meet the new route from Paragon station. The straight line passes across Hessle and Anlaby roads on the level, the latter where the tram shed was to the south on the right hand side and where

Hull Paragon Signals *Photo. ex LNER*
The entrance to Paragon Station, seen when the new signal box was under construction, left, and looking down the long slip line which ran across all running lines. The outward signals are neatly underslung beneath the gantry. Note the large 'Hull' sign and 'end of house' advert.

a small cabin on the west side controlled the gates adjacent to wooden platforms which appeared later for Hull Fair excursions. Newington platform received trains which would empty and then run on either to Dairycoates or to Beverley for servicing and stabling. One wonders where the first excursion mentioned above would have deposited its passengers. A second small box 'Waterworks' on the east side, controlled the crossing over Springbank. Here a narrow gauge line ran off to the west for a good way to the eponymous Hull Waterworks.

The new station in Hull, called Paragon Street at first after the nearby road, then shortened to Paragon when it was realised that 'Paragon St. Stn.' would look silly on a timetable, was a fine example of the latest design, set at the west end of the commercial side of the city. The station premises, fully described in the author's 'Railways of Hull' ran east to west along the south side of the lines and were designed by the same G T. Andrews, built of Anston stone, just as the Houses of Parliament were. The train shed, as at the first station had four tracks, the small turntables and two flanking platforms. To the north and attached to the main building was a three road engine shed, while facing east at the buffer stops end was the Station Hotel of 80 bedrooms, where the Queen and Albert stayed for the Grand Opening, a further cause of great excitement, speeches and conviviality.

At Dairycoates a new line was led in towards the centre, flying over the old line and crossing Hessle road on the flat, as well as four more level crossings to reach the new station without any intervening halt on the way. The old straight line was used for excursions to and from the coast which did not wish to stop in Hull, and largely slumbered during the week, except for an occasional bout of activity to surprise road traffic. Paragon was of course enlarged at various times, especially around 1908, with a new frontage facing east to accompany the hotel alongside. The old premises survive to date, though a shoe box set of offices constructed in the 60s to replace an ironwork and glass porte cochere is set to disappear in due course. The old booking office is worth a look and survives complete, though empty, tiles and all. It is virtually impossible to do justice to all the changes which were made in trackwork and signalling over the years, and one has often to make do with the older Ordnance Survey sheets which can be hard to come by, usually for either around 1910 or 1928, so that these will decide what details to offer. Just before the last war, however, there was a massive resignalling, when all the mechanical material went, to be replaced by electrically worked points and signals.

Leaving Paragon station the line heads westwards past the old Girls' High School and Londesborough Barracks on the right, and West Parade House and the workhouse and hospital complex on the left. The first overbridge carries Park street, formerly a level crossing with the signal box beyond; here the running lines become six as far as the second bridge carrying Argyle street where there may have been a level crossing prior to the large scale improvements of 1908. West Parade signal box, a large one, was in the fork of the junction here, left hand line to Selby, centre for Bridlington and right the Victoria Dock line to Hornsea and Withernsea. Before the bridge the lines had sorted themselves out by means of a handsome double scissors crossover, giving two lines for each direction, while two lines ran round the edge of the Victoria Dock line into Botanic Gardens shed, a roundhouse. Following the Bridlington route, we soon crossed a right angled crossing on the flat, the Anlaby Loop which linked the Victoria Dock line to that to Selby and formed a handy turning place for light engines.

Over this flat crossing which needed a signal box of shed like appearance, a facing connection led into the carriage sidings and depot which continued alongside as far as Walton Street crossing, set on a skew requiring very long gates, fitted in LNER days with motors driving tyres to assist opening and closing. From about the same period, 1930, the signal box here was a tall affair with its top section

Walton Street crossing, looking towards Hull. Note the cantilevered signal box and line from Springhead descending on the right.
Photo. C T Goode

cantilevered out over the lines and not unlike the preserved one at Grosmont on the NYMR.

Beyond Walton Street the double track ran up to join the straight line at Cottingham South Jc, first, however, sending up a short spur to the left to join with the former Hull & Barnsley main line which passes over at this point. The spur would be used to send engines requiring repair to Springhead works nearby, or simply to transfer traffic between the two systems. Our line runs round to the north, past the Ideal Boilerworks and sidings which had at one time its own steam locomotive, the outlet for traffic to a projection ran for some distance to the east, arriving eventually at the H & B's Ella Street Jc. and serving the coal depot there and National Wool sheds. Cottingham South was rather a misnomer, as it was quite some distance from the village only some 1 m. 59 ch. further on. The line crosses the main road over the cutely named crossing of “Thwaite Gates’ with its small wooden cabin, to reach the station (4 miles from Paragon) of twin parallel platforms, footbridge at the south end and station buildings of NER suburban style on the left, facing the driveway to the large village. The nearest object of interest is the large and fine church of St. Mary’s. North of the station on the left was a small goods yard dealing chiefly in coal and timber, while the signal box, Cottingham North was some distance away, also on the left, to control the road crossing.

Two memories of Cottingham survive. In the 60s when it was rumoured that Beeching was about to close this particular line, the station suddenly had a visit from workmen who carefully installed a set of smart gas lighting with shining copper pipes to replace the usual paraffin type. Actually,

Old photograph of Cottingham station with train for Hull approaching.
Photo. Lens of Sutton

such odd actions were not unusual, as if times of stress induced them. Parts of the old Hull & Barnsley were painted and given new stretches of wooden fencing, for instance. The other was the grumpy stationmaster at Cottingham who disliked trainspotters:- whenever my young son and I appeared, he would appear as if from nowhere and, short of ordering us both off, would tell us not to leave our footmarks in his flower beds, the station gardens competitions being still in force. Just under 1/2 mile from here was Waterworks ground frame which controlled two sidings on the left with a line off to the Hull Waterworks pumping station, a considerable distance, where it divided into three. This would most likely be the site of Cottingham Moor signal box (5 m.) which closed in August 1936, though this was certainly not open in 1928 as such. The next box north was Beverley Parks on the left, a block post which worked a road crossing with a minor road and a crossover. Sitting in the dmu. behind the driver on the morning run to Bridlington I was surprised to see the home signal at danger and the gates closed to us, very unusual at this place. It was even more surprising to note that the driver had evidently noticed too late and applied his brakes fully. The unit managed to stop with the nearer gate taken in front of it into the middle of the road.

Beverley station, with overall roof and fine covered footbridge.
Photo. C T Goode

With great speed driver, guard and signalman leapt into action and removed the wrecked gate section, retiring into the box to fill in what was needed in the log book. My feeling of apprehension before the accident was most unpleasant. Soon the Minster is impressively visible on the left as the line enters Beverley, crossing on the level first Flemingate with its small cabin to the right, then the road at the station to enter beneath the overall roof of Beverley (8 m.). The signal box here is still on the south side virtually beneath the roof, and currently works the four level crossings and their barriers in the immediate area with the aid of a bank of video screens. The overall roof, one of several in the region, has been well preserved, along with front buildings on the town side (left), while both platforms have been raised to the acceptable modern level by the insertion of an intermediate brick wall. Beverley itself is a short walk from the railway which divides the commercial from the industrial and mass housing area. The centre of the town is worth a visit, with two fine churches and two market places, as well as a traditional market cross, Beverley was the terminus of short workings from Hull, giving the town and Cottingham a regular service. Trackwise, there was as siding on the left between Flemingate and the station crossing, a well as a crossover at each end of it to facilitate the run-round of terminating trains. Beyond the station an extra line on the left ran from the coal yard of four lines from a trailing crossover, over Cherry Tree level crossing and its signal box, left, where there was a further trailing connection and crossover to a further five sidings with a warehouse, down to the next crossing of the Hornsea road, before which it trailed in. Beyond this crossing was Beverley North Jc., left, where the York line took off. In the other direction was an Up loop which ran to the entrance to the station, at the throat of a sizeable yard with two long standage sidings and four dead end roads. A continuation of the sidings wandered behind the station over the station crossing to trail in. Until the end of the sixties this outlet was controlled by one of the early crossbar signals which rotated to show its thinnest side when 'clear'. Before being taken away it managed to receive a shiny coat of paint. At about this time also, during a very hot spell, the loop could be seen in a buckled state over much of its length, more than likely after its use had been discontinued.

Beverley North Jc. was straightforward, with the York line of 1865 going away to the west and the Wolds. On my travels during the sixties on the Brid. line I remember on dark mornings in winter my usual train, the 7.40 am. dmu. from Hull coming to a sudden halt when the driver realised that he had been signalled for the York line in error and was well round the curve. A hasty discussion ensued with the guard who went back to the box to receive orders. After a short delay the dmu. was reversed carefully beyond the road crossing and a fresh start was made. A two man error, one might say, and one wonders how much of the incident was written down.

Old rotating signal at Beverley. *Photo. C T Goode*

BEYOND BEVERLEY

Into the sticks now as the line runs north to curve round the airfield at Leconfield close by to reach Arram (11 1/4 m.) The platforms are staggered, that is, one each side of the level crossing and beyond it in each direction to allow stopping trains to run clear and passengers crossing to walk behind them. The station building was on the east side, a G. T. Andrews structure in the ordinary style. The small signal box opposite was a gatebox only, opposite a single siding and with a crossover. Arram village is a small collection of houses with little to offer. Still on a gently curve which reverses direction once more as we pass through was the station of Lockington (13 m.) with a prime station building of pillared entrance facing the road on the west side and, over the level crossing beyond the signal box on the west side parallel platforms with a crossover between them. Beyond, on the west side also was a two road yard. Lockington was an oddity, firstly because it closed before any of the others, much in the same way that Hemingbrough did on the Selby line, and secondly, perhaps because of the first reason, because it served hardly anywhere, its namesake being nearly two miles away over the main road.

Arram station, looking south. *Photo. Lens of Sutton*

Atmosphere at Arram. *Photo. C T Goode*

A mile further on was Kilnwick, with road crossing, siding on the left, and a crossover worked by a small cabin on the right. Here there was a magnificently tall, slotted home and distant signal which was quite a feature in this isolated place. The distant might have worked from the next crossing at Watton, also a ground frame controlling a siding on the left. Both places would have been convenient for farmers to load up produce directly from the fields in season. Watton was

Somehow the signal box at Lockington seems to be in the wrong place, set too close to the station building. *Photo. K Hoole Collection*

sufficiently near to the village to have justified a halt, one might have thought, though nothing was every built. Visible here on the left in winter is Watton Abbey, partly ruined but with a 15th century house still inhabited, complete with its own ghost.

An up-to-date view of Hutton Cranswick. *Photo. C T Goode*

Hutton Cranswick station is next (16 1/4 m.), beyond the road crossIng, with parallel platforms and standard signal box and station building on the west side, a short way from the village green in Cranswick, the larger of the two places, Hutton lying to the north and nearer the main road. There is quite a lot of new housing appearing in the area. North of the station on the west side was a neat yard layout of two sidings running almost to the road, with goods shed and yard extension beyond the crossover and a single slip, all at a distance from the signal box and so provided with a ground frame.

Class VI 2•6•2T enters Driffield on the 1.22 p.m. Hull-Scarborough in August 1959. *Photo N. Stead*

DRIFFIELD TO BRIDLINGTON

Soon the line begins its turn northeast towards the sea and enters Driffield (19 1/2 m.), a busy and happy little place with its High street running northwest from the station, possessing a wide range of shops, restaurants and hostelries of all kinds. At one time on summer Saturdays the road was divided by a steady stream of traffic to the coast in the morning and back again in the evening, so that it was difficult to cross. The railway was busy then, but at least it knew its place. To the south of the station was a mix of canal wharf, two large houses, 'Grove Cottage' and 'Southorpe Lodge' in their own grounds, a goods station and cattle cake mills. The track layout through Driffield was an easy, though complicated one to fathom on paper, with Driffield Jc. first from the south taking in the lines from Market Weighton and Malton, an additional touch being a turntable on the left just on the curve of the branch itself where a short spur ran off to the end of the signal box. Next came Up and Down single

An old view of Driffield station from the south, with wind screen and overall roof. The gateman poses by his box, and behind the slotted signal is a ridiculously ornate lamp bracket. *Photo. Lens of Sutton*

Road transport waits in Driffield station yard. *Photo. Lens of Sutton*

sidings for odd purposes, such as the storage of motive power off excursions to Bridlington on summer Saturdays - 'Royal Scot' was to be seen resting here on day's outing from Farnley Jc. near the end of its life, and then an important road crossing for local traffic at Driffield Station Gates, a natty little wooden affair like Thwaite Gates found earlier down the line. This cabin was just outside the station itself, with parallel platforms and an overall roof which, in someone's wisdom was removed in 1947 and replaced by unlovely canopies. This meant that the comfort of services, tea room and bookstall all faded away. The track layout through the area is better studied from the diagram at the end of this work, along with the others; there was a substantial station yard, crane and coal depot along the west side, with goods sidings on the east. As at Beverley there was a long Up relief line which began at Meadow Gates box, while the parallel Down additional line was for goods only, running from the siding, though this joined well to the north of the station towards Meadow Gates. The signal box controlling the yard activities was Wansford, on the left with supervision of the road to Hornsea. As Wansford village is

A view of Nafferton station, looking towards Driffield, with staff and passengers on view. The signal box is the original, smaller version.
Photo. Lens of Sutton

two or more miles from this point it is hard to understand why the name was chosen, when 'Driffield North' would have done very nicely.

Nafferton station today. *Photo. C T Goode*

The original goods shed, Nafferton. *Photo. C T Goode*

Between Driffield and Bridlington the landscape has a different aspect, more of a rolling character between the Wolds and the coast, though the latter is too far away to catch more lthan a glimpse of sea. The road fairs better in this respect and is also flat, apart from bumps near Ruston Parva and Burton Agnes. Out of Driffield and the line turns north east to reach Nafferton first of all (21 1/2 m.), a large village to the north of the line. On that side was met first a largish yard of five sidings adjacent to a flour mill, which would have to be shunted into the long headshunt and then presumably over the slip and off for the Driffield direction. Another main to main crossover would have allowed an engine to run round its wagons if the Bridlington direction were needed, but the layout seemed lacking in this respect. On the right hand side a single line ran to the large NER standard goods shed which still survives here. Over the level crossing with the signal box on the right were the parallel platforms and larger station design with the pillars in front, on the left facing the roadway. The next station was Lowthorpe (23 3/4 m.) another rather odd naming, since the small village was some distance away to the west, while a much larger

A neat clutter at Burton Agnes, looking towards Bridlington. The building left is the original signal box. *Photo. K Hoole Collection*

village, Harpham was at a similar distance to the north, but obviously did not deserve the honour of having a station named after it. There was not much distinctive about Lowthorpe, only a Down siding and goods shed on the left opposite the Up platform, then the level crossing and Down platform which was staggered. The Up siding and small yard were beyond, on the outside of the curve, as the line now turned more to the north. The road crossing would be worked manually from the lineside as the signal box was set by the exit to the Down siding and crossover, with a good view up and down the line. The layout changed in due course. After a run of under two miles the line, still running north, reached Burton Agnes (25 ½ m.) a prettily named village lying in the curve and dip of the main road about one mile to the north, with its well-known stately home, seat of the Wickham-Boyntons. Though smallish, the station layout was 'proper', that is with, first an Up siding and cattle dock on the left, road crossing and signal box on the right, next

Lowthorpe has less to show nowadays than anywhere on the line. The remains of the down platform are shown, while behind the camera are two ordinary homes and a goods shed, all in non railway use.

Photo C.T. Goode

parallel platforms with main building on the right, unusually away from the village side and station yard beyond this, with coal drops. Two crossovers, one at each end, enabled running round of trains to take place and the owner of the Big House,Sir Marcus did, into the 60s, order special stops and special trains to take his steeds to and from race meetings. I can recall a morning special of serveral horse boxes, hauled by a Bridlington VI, delaying us at Driffield as it took the Market Weighton line. Even more interesting for its rarity was the time when the 6.40 pm. from Bridlington, a Craven's dmu. which had made its normal halt at Burton Agnes, drew ahead and reversed into the Down siding to pick up a tail load, (a horse box,) more than likely without the extra horse power. It was quite usual for the dmus. to take tail loads about during the Christmas period, when the extra mail went into long wheelbase parcels vans. They seemed to cope with these without any reduction in speed.

Almost at Bridlington now, but with one final station to visit

Looking towards Bridlington the remaining platforms today at Carnaby along with the station houses. The old signal box has been demolished and road closed, a new house built in its place along with the road moved further southwest. *Photo D. Forth*

as the line now turns more eastwards in lightly rolling country to reach Carnaby (28 1/2 m.), a forlorn spot with, at one time nothing but fish ponds to keep it company and its village at a distance to the north. All that was here was a level crossing, signal box on the left and parallel platforms, the rather basic building being on the 'wrong' side, away from the village. There was only one crossover to operate, though during the last war takings at the station were perhaps greater than almost anywhere else on the line, and one wonders whether the airfield's role as an emergency field for damaged or lost aircraft would actually generate so much traffic. Perhaps there was some sort of hush-hush factory in operation in the 1943-45 period. Who knows? In any event, the airfield closed, to be replaced by the sight of a line of Thor guided missiles in the 1960s, all facing east except one, which was probably somebody's joke. The Americans reclaimed them and the site was given over to Ladas instead.

Carnaby signal box, with station clock attached. *Photo. C T Goode*

GROWTH OF BRIDLINGTON

Soon the outskirts of Bridlington are in sight, and the station is reached (30 3/4 m.). The original station at Bridlington was of two platforms, roofed over, with the main run of buildings on the south side towards the Quay. The present day's bridges were a level crossing and an underpass, and beyond the latter towards the station was a two road engine shed on the right which had a simple run in. Opposite this were three sidings, with a facing entry off the running line, then the platform, beyond which the Down line from Hull carried on as the main Up line to Hull which now produced the new Down arrival line over a facing point. The old Up line ran on parallel, to end at buffers by Quay Road crossing. Alongside this, in turn, was a large goods shed which still exists, the line running through it ending as a run-round on the aforesaid old Up line. Beyond the platforms

Bridlington station approach, with excursion on the left.
Photo. C T Goode

Looking south from Bridlington from platforms 1 and 2. The scissors crossing is evident, as are the gantries and large South signal box.
Photo. C T Goode

was a neat scissors crossing to give access to any required running line. An interesting feature was the branch to the Docks, a long single line which ran round behind Windsor Crescent and was worked by a ground frame which later controlled the station goods yard. The branch lasted from 1851-66 and traces of its run still remain in the configuration of the streets built along it. The line was not finally lifted until 1917.

The 1893 view of the station is much as initially, with the layout tidied up and the Up and Down lines running through as one might expect. There was now a further, single road loco. on the north side complete with turntable next to Quay Road signal box which seems to have been there from the start.The run of buildings on the south side was longer, to be joined by the improved overall roof in 1910. Where the Town Hall now stands was a large property, called at first

The interior of Bridlington South signal box. *Photo. C T Goode*

'Roseville', then 'White Lodge', while the gardens around changed names from 'Midway Green' to 'Victoria Gardens'. Soon a large signal box of 120 levers was to appear on the north side, south end, with all the panoply of the 'big' NER, two impressive signal gantries, a three road engine shed and turntable. Back towards Hull, beyond Bessingby bridge was a point where the four running lines which had been created joined into two, the spurs running on for a fair distance as five reception sidings for the holiday traffic.

The excursion island platforms. The train, headed by a B1, was a return summer season weekday excursion to Doncaster, first stop Brough.
Photo. C T Goode

Bridlington shed, right, with water tank left, and turntable and South signal box ahead. *Photo. C T Goode*

Unless one happened to live through the developments at a place such as Bridlington, it is hard to pin down dates of change. At some time platforms Nos. 1 & 2 had 3 & 4 added, with 2 & 3 an island with the remains of the old roof support bases thereon. No.5 was built parallel to No. 4 to which the gated and wide entrance from the new concourse led. No. 5 and new bay No. 6 were added in 1910-11, the bay being easily accessible beyond the new barriers off the concourse. Nos. 7 & 8 were excursion platforms for summer use, devoid of buildings but with access across the station from the main footbridge. Original Nos. 1 & 2 were taken up in 1983, being without the roof which had gone in 1960. Nos. 7 & 8 were originally carriage sidings. The concourse had a booking section which was less than the size of the toilets available!

UPHILL TO FILEY

The run of the line is by no means over, and the more exciting and scenic part of the journey begins with a 1 in 92 climb almost out of the station for 5 1/2 miles to Speeton, a taxing gradient for the crew of any tired work horse which had, perhaps, already climbed the Wolds through Enthorpe. Gresley's new D49s must have had trouble from time to time, as they were prone to slip in such circumstances. During the time of the first World War the line was singled, the track taken away for use elsewhere, and it was not until about 1922 that it was decided to restore the deficit. The section north of Bridlington was never as busy as the Hull side. Today, the same still applies, with single stretches to Hunmanby and from Filey to Seamer. The first stop from Bridlington was Flamborough, originally Marton for

Happy family. Sewerby Gates box was the first crossing out of Bridlington going north. In the 60s the man on the last shift who lived in Hull would hastily close down after the passage of the final Scarborough - Hull dmu, then pedal like mad to Bridlington to catch it before it left at 9.15pm. - it always had a ten minute halt! *Photo. K Hoole Collection*

Flamborough station building after closure. Photo. K Hoole Collection

Flamborough (33 1/4 m.), as Marton village was close by; however, the name was in use elsewhere, whereas Flamborough, though further off to the east, supplied the fish traffic and the tourist attractions. Here the line runs due north and south, and the station was encountered first with parallel platforms, then road crossing and signal box on the left. The station buildings were on the right hand side with a largish yard of three sidings and run-round facilities, while a slip crossed to the left to a long and rambling siding which served a quarry.

After a single mile the line reaches Bempton, a large village which is visible close by, the station buildings being on the right by the level crossing, with two parallel platforms and a couple of sidings beyond, also to the right. Railway records show an RAF establishment of some kind here, though from maps it was certainly not an airfield. At this point the line now follows a straight line north-west to reach Speeton (37 1/4 m.), and here on good days one can enjoy

Bempton station, Hull end. The long, open waiting shed is interesting, while the main building is behind the camera, left.

Photo. Lens of Sutton

excellent views of cliff and sea not far distant. Speeton station was situated where the line runs east-west on a wild and bleak hilltop, with the edge of the Wolds and the distant mast on Staxton hill visible for some time to come. Between the railway and the sea a minor coast road leaves the main route at Reighton, to run through Speeton and Bempton villages, ending at Flamborough. On the main A165 the line crosses by a high embankment and a brick bridge, a good place for the winter snows to linger and block up traffic - this has in the past provided much extra trade for the handy 'Dotterel' Inn nearby. As might be expected, the layout at Speeton was rudimentary, with a single siding for coal on the right hand side, then the level crossing and set of parallel platforms. G. T. Andrews buildings survived on this section of route, even running to a pillared portico at Bempton

Hunmanby is almost the same in appearance from this viewpoint as Bempton, save for the short waiting shed. *Photo. Lens of Sutton*

By the time the line has reached Hunmanby (41 1/2 m.) it has come round to a north-east direction once more and reached an interesting track layout and a large village spread around it. Ahead of the statutory level crossing, on the left side was a single siding with a run-off for each direction with, beyond, parallel platforms and the siding for the standard large goods shed on the left. To the right were four sidings with a private line linking them in two places to a large brickworks, the greater portion of which was prominent in the station yard. On the side of the hill to the west is the Hunmanby Girls' School, which generated several daily commuters from as far south as Hutton Cranswick in the 1960s.

Speeton station, with B1 No. 61092 approaching on an express.
Photo. K Hoole Collection

From just before Speeton station the line has been descending at between 1 in 112 and 106, with easier intervals between, and comes down to 1 in 228 to reach Filey, entering the station on a rise of 1 in 166 for a short way. Between Hunmanby and Filey was one of the LNER's last flings - the holiday camp station for Butlin's installed in 1946-7 and opened with old fashioned ceremony on 10th May 1947. There were four platform faces on two islands, each of 900 ft. with run-round lines to the outer and inner faces and a subway beneath the road directly into the camp itself. At the outer ends all came neatly together and went off again in two directions, Up and Down lines forming a triangular junction with the Bridlington line, the north point at Royal Oak North, the other at the South box adjacent to the sewage works, with the third signal box at the station end of the triangle. The whole site was reminiscent of an early Hornby 00 station set, with neat concrete structures and upper quadrant signals, all carefully regimented. Unmanned

Hunmanby station, looking towards Filey. *Photo. K Hoole Collection*

during the week, the three signal boxes and stations were worked by relief staff on Saturdays during the season. Traffic was heavy, with weekly excursions arriving from London Manchester, Leeds, York, Sheffield, Worcester and Newcastle and most points between. One of the rare accidents on the line occurred here when a K3. No. 61846 left Bridlington without the vacuum brake pipe coupled up to the train, due to an oversight. On trying to apply the brakes on the curve into the new station the driver found he had no control and managed to spring off with his fireman before the engine went through the buffers and on to the platform. The new layout lay only a short distance outside Filey and appears to have had little effect on the resort by its visitors, though providing good seasonal work for the locals. The line closed in the 70s, along with the camp, which has been for a long time a forlorn heap of rubble.

Filey, interior view to south with footbridge. *Photo. C T Goode*

Filey is a rather jolly sort of multum in parvo, where everything jostles everything else. The railway has been chiefly responsible for this, standing guard at the sole entry and exit at the station level crossing. All the newer building, including the comprehensive school, has taken place to the west of the line, while on the other side Station road takes one down through the shop to the sea, with a steep hill at the end, while West avenue runs past several wealthy looking residences. To the north is a pleasantly deep ravine which takes the visitor down to the boat landing while if one stays aloft a footpath leads round to the Brigg, a shortish promontory accessible on both sides to the beach below when the tide is out. Though not as gleaming white as the cliffs at Bridlington, the Brigg, of boulder clay is nearer to the town and enjoys distant views of Whitby and and Scarborough nearby. A tale worth telling is that the Devil set out one day to make a bridge over the North Sea for some good reason known only to himself, but gave up, leaving the Brigg, or bridge, as the sum total of his efforts.

Filey, opposite direction with signal box. *Photo. C T Goode*

Filey's (44 1/4 m.) station coal yard was neat, with the town gas works in the same area and even the water works close by. Three sidings served the site, on the right before the station is reached, worked by a ground frame some 369 yd. from the station signal box. The station itself is of Up and Down lines, covered by an overall roof similar to Driffield and had at one time a short bay out in the open air on the Down side north end, which was probably used for holding the railbus during its period of short workings. All the roofed over stations were of the same pattern, and during the 1980s someone decided that the covering of this one could be removed by stealth in the hope that nobody would notice - possibly the person who had been active at the Brigg many years earlier. Thus, a chunk at the south end disappeared, exposing the footbridge which ran across internally beneath the roof line. However, after being left in a tatty state for some time, new thoughts appeared at head office and it was decided that a 'makeover' should happen, so replacing the purloined section and producing the cleaner, neater station

Filey, station frontage. *Photo. C T Goode*

which is to be seen today. Across the level crossing was the station yard to the right with sidings and access to the goods shed and a run-round available in the yard or over slips on the running lines.

THE FINAL STAGE TO SEAMER

The line now leaves Filey running north-east, and the journey is almost over as the route takes a sinuous, mainly westerly course to reach Gristhorpe (46 1/4 m.), a lowly place with its signal box originally to the left at the road crossing, parallel platforms, then single siding and yard on the left and a crossover to complete things. It is interesting that Gristhorpe, a village about half a mile to the north, had its station booking office on the far side of the line, instead of nearer as was usual. At 48 miles, further on was Cayton, even more lowly with parallel platforms and station building on the correct side for the village, a large one strung out along the road nearby and signal box on the same side with no trackwork to be seen in any yard. Apparently, for many years the station was run by a stationmistress, no doubt a pleasant sinecure, especially as the crossing was a minor

Diesel power, possibly a 'Deltic', heads north past the remains of Gristhorpe. *Photo. K Hoole Collection*

Cayton, with its rather faded station building.   *Photo. K Hoole Collection*

back road to Hunmanby. The place would have some appeal to tourists with the beautiful Cayton Bay not far distant. The little wooden signal box is still in use today, while the station buildings survive at Gristhorpe, similar in style to some found on the Wensleydale branch. At 50 $\frac{3}{4}$ m. the line reaches Seamer Jc., still mechanically operated at present, together with the Station box. This is dealt with in the author's 'Yorkshire & Scarborough Railway, uniform with this work. An up-to-date touch is that the traveller, if in need of refreshment, can now repair either to the new hotel or the fine supermarket just across the road from Seamer station - places unheard of here until recently!

Filey Holiday Camp station. In the foreground is the road train used to ferry the customers to the site, seemingly ignored here by the arrivals. The 2•6•0 loco is awaiting its next stint of double -heading duty. The neat signalling can be seen to the rear. *Photo. K Hoole Collection*

HOW THEY RAN

1851

Looking at the back issues of 'Bradshaw's Timetable' in 1851, when the trains would leave from Kingston Street in Hull, there were four trains each on weekdays and one on Sundays, these leaving Hull as follows:

8.15am., 12.45pm., 4.00 and 6.30pm.

and Scarborough at

6.45am., 9.10am., 2.00pm. and 5.35pm

The 4pm. did not stop at Lowthorpe and Carnaby, the 2pm. not stopping at Cayton, Gristhorpe, Speeton, Bempton, Carnaby and Lowthorpe. The overall running time from end to end for the stopping trains was 2 3/4 hours. The Sunday train was all-stations from Hull dep. 8.15am., arrive Bridlington at 9.45, returning at 3pm., arriving in Hull at 4.30.

One of the former 'crack' H & B passenger engines, 4•4•0 No. 2425 leaves Cottingham on an evening train to Bridlington. *Photo. T Rounthwaite*

1861

Already by 1861 the timetable was becoming more ambitious with trains leaving Hull at 6.20am., 12.30pm. and 4.45 all stations to Scarborough, and returning from there at 6.30am., 11.25, and 4.35pm., the latter pepped up with 'stops by request' here and there. Additional extras were interesting. There was the 10am. from Hull to Driffield which returned to Hull at 11.10 after twenty minutes. Likewise, a train left Hull at 2pm. for Beverley with a similar turn-round, returning at 2.30pm. Oddments were a Tuesdays Only train from Hull to Beverley at 4.20pm. and 6.30pm. and last service at 7.30pm. all stations to Bridlington, with an all-station service Bridlington to Hull at 4pm. An unbalanced late service left Beverley for Hull at 8pm. The Sunday train left Hull for Scarborough at 7am. all stations, and left on the home run at 3.20pm.

1880

By 1880 refinements had crept into the timetable, which was beginning to look towards those of fifty years later. Fares were now quoted: the single 3rd Class Hull-Bridlington was 2/6d (10 1/2p), while that to Scarborough was 4/5 1/2d (22 1/2p). An extra line gave the times of connecting trains to or from Leeds. The idea of a number of short workings to Beverley throughout the day was now brought in, and times are shown below, though these did not always return immediately;

Hull Dep: 6.36am., 9.35, 12.40pm., 2.15, 3.10, 5.30, 7.15, 10.55 to Beverley.

Beverley Dep: 8.12am., 9.50, 11.27, 2.45pm., 3.45, 5.42, 7.45, 9.22, 11.20 to Hull.

Scarborough Dept:
left Hull at 6.20 am., 8.15, 11.15, 1.45pm., 4.45 and 6.15.

Stopping trains still took 2 3/4 hours. The 8.15am. ran non-stop to Driffield after Beverley, reaching Bridlington in the hour, then stopping at Marton, Filey and Seamer to reach Scarborough another hour later, at 10.15am. The earlier Tuesday Only service to Beverley now left at 4pm., now an all-stations to Bridlington, arriving at 5.30pm.

The 4.55pm. ran express from Beverley to Driffield, then to Bridlington in 55 min., then on to Filey and Scarborough, where it arrived at 6.30pm., covering the whole run in 1 3/4 hours. Things were looking up!

In the opposite direction six trains left Scarborough as follows: 6.10am., 8.00, 11.30, 2.45pm., and 7.15, in some cases the stoppers now seemed to cover the ground in 2 1/2 hours, probably due to better motive power. The star performer here was the 8am., which stopped only at Filey, Driffield, Beverley and Cottingham, reaching Hull at 9.38am. The 5pm. was semi-fast, reaching Hull at 7.15pm.

Better were the short turns to Beverley, omitting the through trains mentioned above:

Hull Dep: 6.36am., 9.35, 12.40pm., 2.15, 3.10, 5.30, 7.15 and 10.55 to Beverley.

Beverley Dep: 8.12am., 9.50, 11.27, 2.45pm., 3.45, 5.42, 7.45, 9.22 and 11.22 to Hull.

On Sundays the statutory trains ran all-stations to Scarborough and return:

Hull dep: 7.0am.

Scarborough dep: 4.45pm.

This time with two short workings to Beverley:

Hull-Beverley	9am. and 8.30pm.
Beverley-Hull	9.30am. and 9pm.

To some readers this aspect of the study of the line may be boring in its attempt to pick out trends and developments over a considerable time. (It is certainly rather tedious to unearth it all and type it!) With these points in mind, some of the later timetables have been printed in full for the reader to pore over, with attendant notes to assist.

1900

On this timetable Bridlington had at last obtained its businessmen's service, one to Hull in 45 min. non-stop and back home again in 40 min. The Sunday train persisted but the Beverley short workings were absorbed into trains travelling further afield. Including the trains on the line to and from York, a separate table gave 25-26 trains each way, with three on Sundays.

1910

Times were much the same as above, though the express between Hull and Bridlington could now manage 40 min. each way. There was little speeding between Bridlington and Scarborough, and trains from Selby via Market Weighton had begun to appear. Services on short runs to and from Beverley had increased to 30-32, with introduction of the latest railcar, the diesel 'autocar'.

1914

The number of trains between Hull and Scarborough now stood at eight or nine each way, with one commendable newcomer, the 4.50pm. ex Hull which ran non-stop to Filey, reaching Scarborough at 6.05pm. There was simply nothing to equal this in the other direction and the timing has probably never been repeated since. The 8.15am. from Bridlington and 5.15pm. from Hull still ran non-stop on weekdays, as did the solitary slow train the length of the line each way on Sundays. There were 33 services between Hull and Beverley.

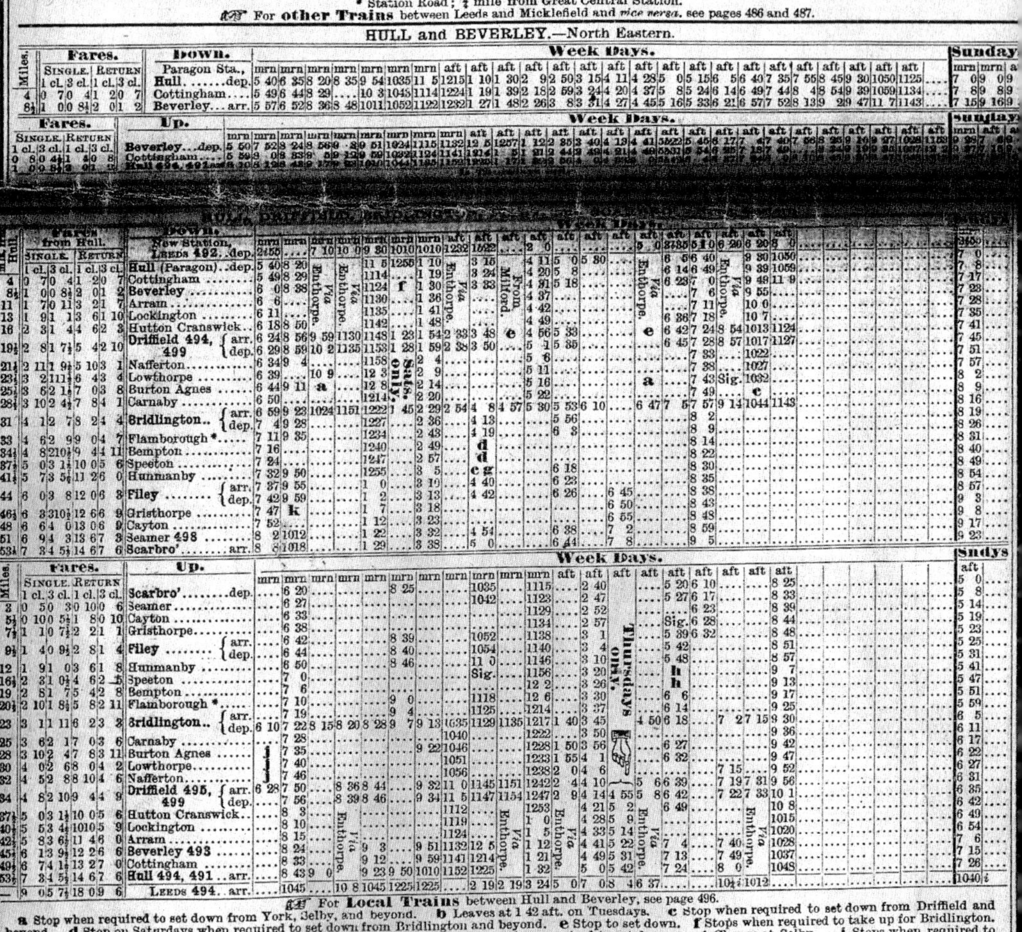

* Station Road; ¾ mile from Great Central Station.

☞ For **other Trains** between Leeds and Micklefield and *vice versa*, see pages 486 and 487.

HULL and BEVERLEY.—North Eastern.

Miles	Single 1 cl.	Single 3 cl.	Return 1 cl.	Return 3 cl.	Down. Paragon Sta.,	mrn	mrn	mrn	mrn	mrn	mrn	mrn	aft	aft	aft	aft	aft	aft	aft	aft	aft	aft	aft	aft	aft	aft	aft	aft	aft		Sunday mrn	Sunday mrn	Sunday a[illegible]
					Hull........dep.	5 40	6 35	8 20	8 35	9 54	1035	11 5	1215	1 10	1 30	2 9	2 50	3 15	4 11	4 28	5 0	5 15	6 5	6 40	7 35	7 55	8 45	9 30	1050	1125	....	7 0	9 0	9
4	0 7	0 4	1 2	0 7	Cottingham....	5 49	6 44	8 29	....	10 3	1045	1114	1224	1 19	1 39	2 18	2 59	3 24	4 20	4 37	5 8	5 24	6 14	6 49	7 44	8 4	8 54	9 39	1059	1134	....	7 8	9 8	9
8½	1 0	0 8½	2 0	1 2	Beverley...arr.	5 57	6 52	8 36	8 48	1011	1052	1122	1232	1 27	1 48	2 26	3 8	3 31	4 27	4 45	5 16	5 33	6 21	6 57	7 52	8 13	9 2	9 47	11 7	1143	....	7 15	9 16	9

Single 1 cl.	Single 3 cl.	Return 1 cl.	Return 3 cl.	Up.	mrn	mrn	mrn	mrn	mrn	mrn	mrn	mrn	mrn	aft	aft	aft	aft	aft	aft	aft	aft	aft	aft	aft	aft	aft	aft	aft	aft	aft	aft	Sunday mrn	Sunday aft	Sunday a[illegible]
				Beverley...dep.	5 50	7 52	8 24	8 56	9 8	9 51	1024	1115	1132	12 5	1257	1 12	2 35	3 40	4 19	4 41	5b22	5 45	6 17	7 4	7 40	7 56	8 26	9 16	9 27	1028	1153	9 28	7 [illegible]	[illegible]
0 8	0 4½	1 4	0 8	Cottingham....	5 59	8 0	8 33	9 5	9 12	9 59	1032	1124	1141	1214	1 5	1 21	2 44	3 49	4 21	4 49	5b31	5 54	6 25	7 13	7 49	....	8 34	9 19	9 36	1037	12 2	9 37	7 15	[illegible]
1 0	0 8½	[illegible]	[illegible]	Hull 494, 491 arr.	[illegible]	[illegible]	[illegible]	[illegible]	[illegible]	[illegible]	[illegible]	[illegible]	[illegible]	[illegible]	[illegible]	[illegible]	[illegible]	[illegible]	[illegible]	[illegible]	[illegible]	[illegible]	[illegible]	[illegible]	[illegible]	[illegible]	[illegible]	[illegible]	[illegible]	[illegible]	[illegible]	[illegible]	[illegible]	[illegible]

HULL, DRIFFIELD, BRIDLINGTON, [illegible]

Miles from Hull	Fares from Hull Single 1 cl.	Single 3 cl.	Return 1 cl.	Return 3 cl.	Down.	mrn	mrn	mrn	mrn	mrn	mrn	mrn	aft	aft	aft	aft	aft	aft	aft	aft	aft	aft	aft	aft	aft	Sundays
					New Station, Leeds 492..dep.	2155	....	7 10	10 0	9 30	1010	1010	1232	1522	....	2 0	....	....	....	5 0	[illegible]	5 10	6 20	6 20	8 0	[illegible]
					Hull (Paragon)..dep.	5 40	8 20	Via Enthorpe.	Via Enthorpe.	11 5	1255	1 10	Via Enthorpe.	3 15	From Milford.	4 11	5 0	5 30	....	Via Enthorpe.	6 5	6 40	Via Enthorpe.	9 30	1050	7 0
4	0 7	0 4	1 2	0 7	Cottingham	5 49	8 29			1114	....	1 19		3 24		4 20	5 8	....	....		6 14	6 49		9 39	1059	7 8
8½	1 0	0 8½	2 0	1 2	Beverley	6 0	8 38			1124	f	1 30		3 33		4 31	5 18	....	....		6 23	7 0		9 49	11 9	7 17
11	1 7	0 11	3 2	1 7	Arram	6 6	....			1130	....	1 36		....		4 37	....	....	....		....	7 6		9 55	....	7 23
13	1 9	1 1	3 6	1 10	Lockington	6 11	....			1135	....	1 41		....		4 42	....	....	....		....	7 11		10 0	....	7 28
16	2 3	1 4	4 6	2 3	Hutton Cranswick	6 18	8 50			1142	....	1 48		....		4 49	....	....	....		6 36	7 18		10 7	....	7 35
19½	2 8	1 7½	5 4	2 10	Driffield 494, 499 arr.	6 24	8 56	9 59	1130	1148	1 23	1 54	2 33	3 48	e	4 56	5 33	....	....	e	6 42	7 24	8 54	1013	1124	7 41
					Driffield dep.	6 29	8 59	10 2	1135	1153	1 28	1 59	2 38	3 50	....	5 1	5 35	....	....	....	6 45	7 28	8 57	1017	1127	7 45
21½	2 11	1 9½	5 10	3 1	Nafferton	6 34	9 4	....	....	1158	Sats. only.	2 4	....	....	....	5 6	....	....	....	....	....	7 33	....	1022	....	7 51
23½	3 2	1 11½	6 4	3 4	Lowthorpe	6 39	....	10 9	....	12 3		2 9	....	....	....	5 11	....	....	....	....	....	7 38	....	1027	....	7 57
25½	3 6	2 1½	7 0	3 8	Burton Agnes	6 44	9 11	a	....	12 8		2 14	....	....	....	5 16	....	....	....	a	....	7 43	Sig.	1032	....	8 2
28½	3 10	2 4½	7 8	4 1	Carnaby	6 50	....	....	....	1214		2 20	....	....	....	5 22	....	....	....	....	....	7 49	....	e	....	8 9
31	4 1	2 7	8 2	4 4	Bridlington.. arr.	6 59	9 23	1024	1151	1222	1 45	2 29	2 54	4 8	4 57	5 30	5 53	6 10	....	6 47	7 5	7 57	9 14	1044	1143	8 16
					Bridlington dep.	7 4	9 28	....	....	1227	....	2 36	....	4 13	....	....	5 56	....	....	....	....	8 2	....	....	....	8 19
33	4 6	2 9	9 0	4 7	Flamborough *	7 11	9 35	....	....	1234	....	2 43	....	4 19	....	....	6 3	....	....	....	....	8 9	....	....	....	8 26
34½	4 8	2 10½	9 4	4 11	Bempton	7 16	....	....	....	1240	....	2 49	....	d	....	....	....	....	....	....	....	8 14	....	....	....	8 31
37½	5 0	3 1½	10 0	5 6	Speeton	7 24	....	....	....	1247	....	2 57	....	d	....	....	....	....	....	....	....	8 22	....	....	....	8 40
41½	5 7	3 5½	11 2	6 0	Hunmanby	7 32	9 50	....	....	1255	....	3 5	....	c g	....	....	6 18	....	....	....	....	8 30	....	....	....	8 49
44	6 0	3 8	12 0	6 3	Filey arr.	7 37	9 55	....	....	1 0	....	3 10	....	4 40	....	....	6 23	....	....	....	....	8 35	....	....	....	8 54
					Filey dep.	7 42	9 59	....	....	1 2	....	3 13	....	4 42	....	....	6 26	....	6 45	....	....	8 38	....	....	....	8 57
46½	6 3	3 10½	12 6	6 9	Gristhorpe	7 47	k	....	....	1 7	....	3 18	....	....	....	....	....	....	6 50	....	....	8 43	....	....	....	9 3
48	6 6	4 0	13 0	6 9	Cayton	7 52	....	....	....	1 12	....	3 23	....	....	....	....	....	....	6 55	....	....	8 48	....	....	....	9 8
51	6 9	4 3	13 6	7 3	Seamer 498	8 2	1012	....	....	1 22	....	3 32	....	4 54	....	....	6 38	....	7 2	....	....	8 59	....	....	....	9 17
53½	7 3	4 5½	14 6	7 6	Scarbro'.......arr.	8 8	1018	....	....	1 29	....	3 38	....	5 0	....	....	6 44	....	7 8	....	....	9 5	....	....	....	9 23

Miles	Fares Single 1 cl.	Single 3 cl.	Return 1 cl.	Return 3 cl.	Up.	mrn	mrn	mrn	mrn	mrn	mrn	mrn	mrn	mrn	mrn	mrn	aft	aft	aft	aft	aft	aft	aft	aft	aft	Sndys aft
					Scarbro'........dep.	....	6 20	....	....	....	8 25	....	....	1035	....	1115	....	2 40	Thursdays only.	....	5 20	6 10	....	....	8 25	5 0
3	0 5	0 3	0 10	0 6	Seamer	....	6 27	....	....	....	....	....	....	1042	....	1123	....	2 47		....	5 27	6 17	....	....	8 33	5 8
5½	0 10	0 5½	1 8	0 10	Cayton	....	6 33	....	....	....	....	....	....	....	....	1129	....	2 52		....	....	6 23	....	....	8 39	5 14
7½	1 1	0 7½	2 2	1 1	Gristhorpe	....	6 38	....	....	....	....	....	....	....	....	1134	....	2 57		....	Sig.	6 28	....	....	8 44	5 19
9½	1 4	0 9½	2 8	1 4	Filey arr.	....	6 42	....	....	....	8 39	....	....	1052	....	1138	....	3 1		....	5 39	6 32	....	....	8 48	5 23
					Filey dep.	....	6 44	....	....	....	8 40	....	....	1054	....	1140	....	3 4		....	5 42	....	....	....	8 51	5 25
12	1 9	1 0	3 6	1 8	Hunmanby	....	6 50	....	....	....	8 46	....	....	11 0	....	1146	....	3 10		....	5 48	....	....	....	8 57	5 31
16½	2 3	1 0½	4 6	2 5	Speeton	....	7 0	....	....	....	....	....	....	Sig.	....	1156	....	3 20		....	h	....	....	....	9 7	5 41
19	2 8	1 7	5 4	2 8	Bempton	....	7 6	....	....	....	....	....	....	....	....	12 2	....	3 26		....	h	....	....	....	9 13	5 47
20½	2 10	1 8½	5 8	2 11	Flamborough *	....	7 10	....	....	....	9 0	....	....	1118	....	12 6	....	3 30		....	6 6	....	....	....	9 17	5 51
					Bridlington.. arr.	....	7 19	....	....	....	9 4	....	....	1125	....	1214	....	3 37		....	6 14	....	....	....	9 25	5 59
23	3 1	1 11	6 2	3 2	Bridlington dep.	6 10	7 22	8 15	8 20	8 28	9 7	9 13	1035	1129	1135	1217	1 40	3 45		4 50	6 18	....	7 2	7 15	9 30	6 5
25	3 6	2 1	7 0	3 6	Carnaby	....	7 28	....	....	....	....	....	1040	....	....	1222	....	3 50		....	....	....	....	....	9 36	6 11
28	3 10	2 4	7 8	3 11	Burton Agnes	j	7 35	....	....	....	....	9 22	1046	....	....	1228	1 50	3 56		....	6 27	....	....	....	9 42	6 17
30	4 0	2 6	8 0	4 2	Lowthorpe	j	7 40	....	....	....	....	....	1051	....	....	1233	1 55	4 1		....	6 32	....	....	....	9 47	6 22
32	4 5	2 8	8 10	4 6	Nafferton	j	7 46	....	....	....	....	....	1056	....	....	1238	2 0	4 6		....	....	....	7 15	....	9 52	6 27
34	4 8	2 10	9 4	4 9	Driffield 495, 499 arr.	6 28	7 50	....	8 36	8 44	....	9 32	11 0	1145	1151	1242	2 4	4 10		5 6	6 39	....	7 19	7 31	9 56	6 31
					Driffield dep.	....	7 56	....	8 39	8 46	....	9 34	11 5	1147	1154	1247	2 9	4 14	4 55	5 8	6 42	....	7 22	7 33	10 1	6 35
37½	5 0	3 1½	10 0	5 6	Hutton Cranswick	....	8 3	....	Via Enthorpe.	....	....	....	1112	....	Via Enthorpe.	1253	Via Enthorpe.	4 21	5 2	Via Enthorpe.	6 49	....	....	Via Enthorpe.	10 8	6 42
40½	5 5	3 4½	10 10	5 9	Lockington	....	8 10	....		....	....	....	1119	....		1 0		4 28	5 9		....	....	....		1015	6 49
42½	5 8	3 6½	11 4	6 0	Arram	....	8 15	....		....	....	....	1124	....		1 5		4 33	5 14		....	....	....		1020	6 54
45½	6 1	3 9½	12 2	6 6	Beverley 493	....	8 24	....		9 3	....	9 51	1132	12 5		1 12		4 41	5 22		7 4	....	7 40		1028	7 6
49½	6 7	4 1½	13 2	7 0	Cottingham	....	8 33	....		9 12	....	9 59	1141	1214		1 21		4 49	5 31		7 13	....	7 49		1037	7 15
53½	7 3	4 5½	14 6	7 6	Hull 494, 491..arr.	....	8 43	9 0		9 23	9 50	1010	1152	1225		1 32		5 0	5 42		7 24	....	8 0		1048	7 26
—	9 0	5 7½	18 0	9 6	Leeds 494..arr.	....	1045	....	10 8	1045	1225	1225	....	2 19	2 19	3 24	5 0	7 0	8 4	6 37	....	....	10[illegible] i	1012	....	1040 i

☞ For **Local Trains** between Hull and Beverley, see page 496.

a Stop when required to set down from York, Selby, and beyond. **b** Leaves at 1 42 aft. on Tuesdays. **c** Stop when required to set down from Driffield and beyond. **d** Stop on Saturdays when required to set down from Bridlington and beyond. **e** Stop to set down. **f** Stops when required to take up for Bridlington. **g** Stops when required to take up for beyond Seamer. **h** Stops on Thursdays when required to set down. **i** Change at Selby. **j** Stops when required to take up for beyond Driffield. **k** Stops when required to take up for York. **l** Leaves at 4 5 aft. on Thursdays.

* 2½ miles to Flamboro' Village, and 3½ miles to Flamboro' Lighthouse.

A page from a 1900 Timetable.

Right: A couple of pages from a 1910 Timetable.

Miles	Down.	mrn	mrn	mrn	mrn	mrn	mrn	mrn	aft	aft	aft	aft	aft	aft	aft	aft
	New Station, 726 Leeds ....dep.	2 54		7 13	9 47	9 35	1015	1015	1225	1 25	1625	2 3	2 3			
—	Hull (Paragon) dp (See below)	5 45	8 5	From Selby, see page 719.		11 5	1250	1 0	Thurs. only.	Except Thursdays.	3 25	From Selby, see page 719.	4 20	4 55	5 30	
4	Cottingham	5 54	8 14			1114		1 9					4 29	5 4		
8¼	Beverley	6 5	8 24			1123	d	1 20			3 39		4 38	5 12		
11¼	Arram	6 11	8 30			1129		1 26					4 44		Except Saturdays.	
13	Lockington	6 16	8 35			1134		1 31					4 49			
16¼	Hutton Cranswick	6 23	8 42			1141		1 38					4 56			
19½	Driffield 719, 720 arr.	6 29	8 48	9 47	1128	1147	1 19	1 44	2 38	3 5	3 54	g	5 2	5 27		
	dep.	6 34	8 51	9 50	1130	1149	1 23	1 49	2 40	3 7	3 56		5 4	5 29		
21¼	Nafferton	6 39	8 56			1154	Sats. only.	1 54					5 10			
23¾	Lowthorpe	6 44		9 56		1159		1 59					5 15			
25¼	Burton Agnes	6 49	9 2	b		12 4		2 4					5 20			
28½	Carnaby	6 54				12 9		2 9					5 25			
30¾	Bridlington ...... arr.	7 3	9 14	1012	1146	1218	1 39	2 18	2 56	3 23	4 12	5 0	5 34	5 45	6 10	
	dep.	7 11	9 17		Via Enthorpe, see page 719.	1222	1 43	2 23	From Selby, see page 719.	From Selby, see page 719.	4 13			5 48		
33½	Flamborough *	7 19	9 25			1230	1 51	2 31			4 21			5 56		
34¾	Bempton	7 25				1236		2 37						a		
37¼	Speeton	7 33				1244		2 45						a		
41½	Hunmanby	7 41	9 40			1252	Sig.	2 53			4 36			6 11		
44¼	Filey .... arr.	7 46	9 45			1257	2 11	2 58			4 41			6 16		
	dep.	7 50	9 48			1259	2 14	3 1			4 42			6 18		6 43
46½	Gristhorpe	7 55	9 53			1 4		3 6								6 48
48	Cayton	7 59	9 57			1 8		3 10								6 52
50¼	Seamer 705, 715	8 5	10 3			1 14		3 16			4 53					6 58
53¼	Scarborough 718 ..arr.	8 14	1013			1 24	2 29	3 26			5 2			6 33		7 6

Down.	aft	aft	aft	aft	aft	aft	Sundays mrn
New Station, 726 Leeds ....dep.	4 57	3 45	4 57	6 35	6 25	8 0	2 54
Hull (Paragon) dp (See below)	From Selby, see page 719.	6 5	6 35	From Selby, see page 719.	9 30	1057	7 0
Cottingham		6 14	6 44		9 39	11 6	7 9
Beverley		6 24	6 54		9 49	1116	7 19
Arram			7 0		9 55		7 25
Lockington			7 5		10 0		7 30
Hutton Cranswick		6 37	7 12		10 7		7 37
Driffield 719, 720 arr.	g	6 44	7 18	8 54	1013	1131	7 43
dep.		6 47	7 20	8 57	1015	1134	7 45
Nafferton			7 25		1020		7 50
Lowthorpe			7 30		1025		7 55
Burton Agnes	b		7 35	Sig.	1029		8 0
Carnaby			7 40		c		8 5
Bridlington ...... arr.	6 55	7 3	7 49	9 15	1041	1150	8 15
dep.			7 52				8 22
Flamborough *			8 0				8 30
Bempton			8 6				8 36
Speeton			8 14				8 44
Hunmanby			8 22				8 52
Filey .... arr.			8 27				8 57
dep.			8 30				9 0
Gristhorpe			8 35				9 5
Cayton			8 39				9 9
Seamer 705, 715			8 45				9 15
Scarborough 718 ..arr.			8 55				9 25

a Stops on Saturdays when required to set down from Bridlington and beyond.
b Set down when required from York, Selby, and beyond.
b Leaves at 1 50 aft. on Tuesdays.
c Stops when required to set down from Driffield and beyond.
d Stops if required to take up for Bridlington and beyond.
g Sets down only.
* 2¼ miles to Flamborough Village, and 3½ miles to Flamborough Lighthouse or the North Landing.

HULL and BEVERLEY.—North Eastern.

Mls	Up.	mrn	mrn	mrn	m	mrn	m	mrn	m	mrn	m	aft	aft	m	aft	aft	m	aft	aft	aft	aft	aft	aft	m
—	Hull (Paragon).dep.	5 45	6 52	8 5	8 15	8 30	8 56	9 53	1030	11 5	1135	12 5	1 0	1 15	1 40	1 55	2 20	3 5	3 25	4 10	4 20	4 55	5 15	5 45
4	Cottingham	5 54	7 1	8 14	8 23	....	9 4	10 1	1038	1114	1143	1214	1 9	1 23	1 48	2 4	2 28	3 13	....	4 19	4 29	5 4	5 23	5 53
8¼	Beverley ......arr.	6 2	7 9	8 22	8 33	8 42	9 13	1013	1048	1121	1153	1222	1 17	1 33	1 59	2 12	2 38	3 24	3 38	4 27	4 36	5 11	5 34	6 4

Up.	aft	aft	Sats. aft	aft	aft	aft	m	aft	m	Sundays mrn	mrn	aft	aft	aft
Paragon Station, Hull ....dep.	6 5	6 35	7 5	7 35	8 20	9 30	10 5	1057	1138	7 0	9 0	2 30	5 45	9 25
Cottingham	6 14	6 44	7 13	7 44	8 28	9 39	1013	11 6	1146	7 9	9 8	2 38	5 53	9 33
Beverley ......arr.	6 22	6 52	7 23	7 52	8 39	9 47	1023	1114	1157	7 17	9 19	2 49	6 3	9 45

Mls	Down.	mrn	mrn	mrn	m	mrn	m	mrn	mrn	m	mrn	mrn	m	aft	aft	m	aft	aft	aft	aft	Thurs. aft	Thurs. aft
—	Beverley ......dep.	5 20	7 54	8 21	8 50	9 4	9 17	9 51	1019	11 0	1115	1155	1224	1 2	1 13	1 55	2 35	3 32	4 6	4 24	5 11	5 42
4¼	Cottingham	5 27	8 1	8 28	8 58	9 12	9 25	9 58	1026	11 8	1122	12 2	1232	1 9	1 20	2 3	2 42	3 39	4 13	4 31	5 19	5 49
8¼	Hull 724, 728, 792	5 37	8 11	8 39	9 9	9 23	9 35	10 8	1036	1118	1133	1213	1242	1 20	1 31	2 13	2 52	3 50	4 24	4 42	5 30	5 59

Down.	Sats. aft	aft	aft	aft	aft	aft	aft	aft	m	m	Sundays mrn	aft	aft	aft	aft
Beverley ......dep	5 48	6 19	7 2	7 34	7 52	8 47	9 23	1024	1053	12 5	9 28	3 0	6 53	7 6	9 55
Cottingham	5 55	6 26	7 10	7 41	....	8 54	9 30	1031	11 1	1212	9 35	3 7	7 0	7 13	10 2
Hull 724, 728, 792	6 6	6 37	7 23	7 52	8 5	9 5	9 41	1042	1111	1222	9 45	3 17	7 12	7 25	1014

m Auto-car.

Miles	Up.	mrn	mrn	mrn	mrn	mrn	mrn	mrn	mrn	mrn	mrn	mrn	aft	aft
	Scarborough ......dep.	To Market Weighton, see page 719.	6 25	Via Enthorpe, see page 719.			8 22				1025	1117		2 30
3	Seamer		6 32									1124		2 37
5½	Cayton		Sig.									1130		2 43
7½	Gristhorpe		Sig.									1134		2 47
9½	Filey .... arr.		6 47				8 36				1040	1139		2 52
	dep.		6 49				8 38				1042	1141		2 54
12½	Hunmanby		6 56				8 44				1049	1148		3 1
16¼	Speeton		7 6								1059	1158		3 11
19¼	Bempton		7 12									12 4		3 17
20½	Flamborough *		7 15				9 0				11 5	12 7		3 20
23	Bridlington ...... arr.		7 21				9 4				1112	1213		3 26
	dep.	6 30	7 24	8 5	8 15	8 30	9 8	9 13	1020	1035	1116	1217	1 30	3 29
25¼	Carnaby		7 29						1025			1222		3 34
28¼	Burton Agnes	d	7 35	h				9 22	1031			1228	1 39	3 40
30	Lowthorpe	d	7 40						1036			1233	1 44	3 45
32¼	Nafferton	d	7 45						1041			1238	1 49	3 50
34¼	Driffield 719, 720 arr.	6 50	7 50	8 23		8 46		9 32	1046	1111	1134	1243	1 54	3 55
	dep.	6 53	7 52	8 26		8 48		9 34	1048	1113	1138	1246	1 59	3 57
37¼	Hutton Cranswick		7 59						1055	To Selby, see page 719.		1253	To Selby, see page 719.	4 4
40¼	Lockington		8 6						11 2			1 0		4 11
42¼	Arram		8 11						11 7			1 5		4 16
45¼	Beverley 712		8 17			9 3		9 49	1113		1153	1 11		4 22
49½	Cottingham		8 28			9 12		9 58	1122		12 2	1 20		4 31
53¾	Hull ‡ 724, 728, 792 arr.		8 39		8 55	9 23	9 45	10 8	1133		1213	1 31		4 42
105¾	724 Leeds (New) ..arr.			9 51	1034			12 6		2 22	2 23	3 19	4 41	6 47

Up.	aft	aft	aft	aft	aft	aft	aft	aft	aft	Sundays aft
Scarborough ......dep.	3 30	Thursdays only.		Saturdays only.	5 17	6 10			8 28	5 0
Seamer	Saturdays only.				5 24	6 17			8 35	5 7
Cayton					5 30	6 23			8 41	5 13
Gristhorpe					5 34	6 27			8 45	5 17
Filey .... arr.	3 44				5 39	6 32			8 50	5 22
dep.	3 46				5 41				8 52	5 24
Hunmanby	3 52				5 47				8 59	5 31
Speeton					5 57				9 9	5 41
Bempton					6 3				9 15	5 47
Flamborough *					6 6				9 18	5 50
Bridlington ...... arr.	4 10				6 13				9 25	5 58
dep.			4 35	5 13	6 17		6 50	7 15	9 29	6 5
Carnaby							6 55		9 34	6 10
Burton Agnes					6 26				9 40	6 16
Lowthorpe					6 31				9 45	6 21
Nafferton							7 6		9 50	6 26
Driffield 719, 720 arr.			4 51	5 29	6 38		7 11	7 31	9 55	6 31
dep.		4 45	4 53	5 31	6 41		7 13	7 33	9 57	6 35
Hutton Cranswick		4 52	Via Enthorpe.		6 48			To Selby, see page 719.	10 4	6 42
Lockington		4 59					Sig.		1011	6 49
Arram		5 4					Sig.		1016	6 54
Beverley 712		5 9		5 46	7 0		7 32		1022	7 0
Cottingham		5 19		5 55	7 10		7 41		1031	7 13
Hull ‡ 724, 728, 792 arr.		5 30		6 6	7 23		7 52		1042	7 25
724 Leeds (New) .. arr.		7 58	6 26				1013	1013		1013

d Stops when required to take up for beyond Driffield.
h Stops when required to take up for Hull, Selby, York, or Malton.
* 2¼ miles to Flamborough Village, and 3½ miles to Flamborough Lighthouse or the North Landing.
‡ Nearly 1 mile to H. & B. (Cannon Street) Station.

∴ For **OTHER TRAINS** between Scarborough and Seamer, see pages 705 and 715.

NORTHALLERTON, BEDALE, LEYBURN, and HAWES JUNCTION.—North Eastern.

Miles	Down.	mrn	mrn	mrn	mrn	aft	aft	aft	aft	aft
	684 York ....dep.	5 55	....	8 45	9 57	1250	....	2 40	5 47	8 5
	Northallerton dep.	7 20	....	9 48	1052	1 38	....	3 55	6 33	9 40
3	Ainderby	7 27	....	9 55	1059	1 45	....	4 2	6 40	9 47
4¼	Scruton	7 31	....	9 59	11 3	1 49	....	4 6	6 44	9 51
5¾	Leeming Bar	7 35	....	10 3	11 7	1 53	....	4 10	6 48	9 55
7½	Bedale	7 41	....	10 7	1113	1 59	....	4 16	6 54	10 1
9¾	Crakehall	7 47	....	....	1119	2 5	....	4 22	7 0	10 7
11¼	Jervaulx	7 54	....	....	1123	2 13	....	4 30	7 5	10 12
13¼	Finghall Lane	7 59	....	....	1128	2 18	....	4 35	7 10	Sig.
14¾	Constable Burton ..	8 3	....	....	1132	2 22	....	4 39	7 14	10 21
16¼	Spennithorne	8 7	....	....	1136	2 26	....	4 43	7 18	k
17¾	Leyburn	8 17	....	....	1146	2 37	....	4 54	7 30	10 27
20	Wensley	8 23	....	....	1151	2 43	....	5 0	7 36	....
22	Redmire	8 28	....	....	1156	2 48	....	5 5	7 41	....
25	Aysgarth	8 35	....	....	12 3	2 55	....	5 12	7 49	....
29½	Askrigg	8 45	....	....	1213	3 5	....	5 22	7 59	....
34	Hawes ....[621	8 54	1010	....	1222	3 14	4 5	5 31	8 8	....
39¾	Hawes Junc. † 620 ar	....	1025	....	1238	....	4 17	5 47	8 25	....

Mls	Hawes Junc. and	mrn	mrn	mrn	mrn	aft	aft	aft	Sn aft
—	Garsdale ....dep.	....	6 42	....	1054	1 5	3 15	6 25	
5¾	Hawes	....	6 55	9 7	11 6	1 17	3 35	6 38	5 30
10¼	Askrigg	....	7 4	9 15	1114	1 25	3 44	6 49	5 42
14¾	Aysgarth	....	7 14	9 24	1123	1 34	3 53	7 0	5 55
17¾	Redmire	....	7 21	9 30	1129	1 41	4 0	7 7	6 2
19¾	Wensley	....	7 26	9 35	1134	1 46	4 5	7 12	6 8
22¼	Leyburn	6 10	7 38	9 44	1144	1 56	4 14	7 25	6 16
23¾	Spennithorne	....	7 42	....	1149	Sig.	4 18	Sig.	....
25¼	Constable Burton ..	Sig.	7 46	9 50	1153	2 5	4 22	7 33	6 22
26¾	Finghall Lane	....	7 49	....	1156	2 8	4 25	7 36	6 25
28¼	Jervaulx	Sig.	7 53	9 56	12 0	2 12	4 29	7 40	6 29
30	Crakehall	Sig.	7 57	....	12 5	2 17	4 34	7 45	6 34
32¼	Bedale	6 29	8 2	10 1	1210	2 22	4 39	7 50	6 39
34	Leeming Bar	6 37	8 10	10 7	1217	2 29	4 46	7 58	6 45
35¼	Scruton	Sig.	8 15	1011	1221	2 33	4 50	8 2	6 49
36½	Ainderby ......[686	6 44	8 20	1015	1225	2 37	4 54	8 6	6 53
39¾	Northallerton .arr.	6 52	8 28	1022	1233	2 45	5 2	8 13	6 59
69¾	686 York ......arr.	8 32	9 10	1128	2 3	3 48	6 10	9 18	9 0

k Stops on Saturdays when required to set down. † Hawes Junction and Garsdale.

HULL, DRIFFIELD, BRIDLINGTON, FILEY, and SCARBOROUGH.—North Eastern.

Miles	Down.	Week Days.																Sundays.
		mrn	mrn	mrn	mrn	mrn	mrn	aft	aft	aft	aft	aft	aft	aft	aft	aft	aft	mrn
						Saturdays only.						Except Saturdays.						
	770 Leeds (New Station) dep.	2 54			9 35	1015	1015	1222	2 5					3 52	4 57	6 55	8 0	2 54
—	Hull (Paragon) dep.	5 50	8 5	9 8	11 5	1250	1 0	3 25	4 8	4 50	4 55	5 30		6 5	6 45	9 30	1055	7 0
4	Cottingham	5 59	8 14		1114		1 9		4 17		5 4			6 14	6 54	9 39	11 6	7 9
8¼	Beverley arr.	6 7	8 22	9 20	1122		1 17	3 38	4 25		5 11			6 22	7 2	9 47	1114	7 17
	Beverley dep.	6 10	8 24	9 21	1124	d	1 20	3 39	4 27		5 12			6 24	7 4	9 49	1115	7 19
11¼	Arram	6 16	8 30		1130		1 26		4 33						7 10	9 55		7 25
13	Lockington	6 21	8 35		1135		1 31		4 38						7 15	10 0		7 30
16¼	Hutton Cranswick	6 28	8 42		1142		1 35		4 45					6 37	7 22	10 7		7 37
19¼	Driffield 762, 765 arr.	6 34	8 48	9 36	1148	1 19	1 44	3 54	4 51		5 27			6 44	7 28	1013	1130	7 43
	Driffield dep.	6 39	8 51	9 37	1150	1 21	1 49	3 55	4 53		5 29			6 46	7 30	1015	1131	7 45
21¼	Nafferton	6 44	8 56		1155		1 54		4 58						7 35	1020		7 50
23¾	Lowthorpe	6 49			12 0		1 59		5 3						7 40	1025		7 55
26¼	Burton Agnes	6 54	9 3		12 5		2 4		5 8						7 45	1030		8 0
28¾	Carnaby	7 1			1212		2 11		5 15						7 52	c		8 7
30¾	Bridlington arr.	7 6	9 12	9 53	1217	1 37	2 16	4 11	5 20		5 45	6 10		7 2	7 57	1040	1147	8 12
	Bridlington dep.	7 13	9 15	9 56	1221		2 21	4 13			5 48				8 0			8 19
33¼	Flamborough *	7 21	9 23		1229		2 29	4 21			5 56				8 8			8 27
34¾	Bempton	7 26			1234		2 34				s				8 13			8 32
37¾	Speeton	7 34			1242		2 42				s				8 21			8 40
41¼	Hunmanby	7 42	9 38		1250		2 50	4 36			6 11				8 29			8 48
44¼	Filey arr.	7 47	9 43	1018	1255		2 55	4 41		5 48	6 16				8 34			8 53
	Filey dep.	7 51	9 46	1019	1257		2 58	4 42		5 51	6 18		6 42		8 36			8 56
46¾	Gristhorpe		9 51				3 3						6 47		8 41			9 1
48	Cayton	8 0	9 55		1 6		3 7						6 51		8 45			9 5
50¾	Seamer 760 and below.	8 5	10 0	1029	1 11		3 12	4 52					6 57		8 50			9 10
53¾	Scarborough 764 arr.	8 14	1010	1038	1 21		3 22	5 2		6 5	6 33		7 7		9 0			9 20

Miles	Up.	Week Days.																	Sundays.
		mrn	mrn	mrn	mrn	mrn	mrn	mrn	mrn	aft	aft	aft	aft	aft	aft	aft	aft	aft	aft
												Thursdays only.						Thursday only.	
	Scarborough dep.	6 20			8 22			1025	1117	1 45	2 30		4 20	5 17	6 12		8 30	11 5	5 0
3	Seamer	6 27							1124	1 52	2 37			5 24	6 19		8 37	1111	5 7
5½	Cayton	Sig.							1130		2 43			5 30	6 25		8 43	1117	5 13
7½	Gristhorpe	Sig.							1134		2 47			5 34	6 29		8 47	1121	5 17
9½	Filey arr.	6 42			8 36			1040	1139	2 1	2 52		4 35	5 39	6 34		8 52	1126	5 22
	Filey dep.	6 44			8 38			1042	1141	2 3	2 54		4 38	5 41			8 54		5 24
12½	Hunmanby	6 51			8 44			1049	1148		3 1			5 48			9 1		5 31
16	Speeton	7 1						1059	1158		3 11			5 58			9 11		5 41
19½	Bempton	7 7							12 4		3 17			6 4			9 17		5 47
20½	Flamborough *	7 11			8 59			11 6	12 8	2 21	3 21			6 8			9 21		5 52
23	Bridlington arr.	7 15			9 3			1110	1212	2 25	3 25		4 58	6 12			9 25		5 56
	Bridlington dep.	7 20	8 15	8 30	9 6	9 13	1020	1116	1217	2 30	3 29		5 2	6 17		6 50	9 30		6 5
25½	Carnaby	7 25					1025		1222		3 34					6 55	9 35		6 10
28¼	Burton Agnes	7 31				9 22	1031		1228		3 40			6 26			9 41		6 16
30	Lowthorpe	7 36					1036		1233		3 45			6 30			9 46		6 22
32½	Nafferton	7 41					1041		1238		3 50			6 35		7 6	9 51		6 27
34½	Driffield 762, 765 arr.	7 46		8 46		9 32	1046	1134	1243	2 46	3 55		5 18	6 40		7 11	9 56		6 32
	Driffield dep.	7 49		8 48		9 34	1048	1138	1246	2 48	3 57	4 45	5 20	6 43		7 13	9 58		6 36
37½	Hutton Cranswick	7 56					1055		1253		4 4	4 52		6 49			10 5		6 43
40¾	Lockington	8 3					11 2		1 0		4 11	4 59	Sig.			Sig.	1012		6 50
42½	Arram	8 8					11 7		1 5		4 16	5 4	5 35			7 26	1017		6 55
45½	Beverley 763 arr.	8 14		9 3		9 49	1113	1153	1 11	3 3	4 22	5 9	5 41	7 1		7 32	1023		7 1
	Beverley dep.	8 21		9 4		9 51	1115	1155	1 13	3 6	4 24	5 11	5 43	7 3		7 34	1025		7 7
49½	Cottingham	8 28		9 12		9 58	1122	12 2	1 20	3 13	4 31	5 19	5 50	7 11		7 41	1032		7 16
53½	Hull : 768, 773, 836 arr.	8 39	8 55	9 23	9 45	10 8	1133	1213	1 31	3 24	4 42	5 30	6 2	7 23		7 52	1043		7 28
105½	768 Leeds (New) arr.		1036			12 9		2 23	3 19	5 10	6 1	7 52				1013			1013

b Leaves at 1 50 aft. on Tuesdays.
c Stops when required to set down from Driffield and beyond.
d Stop when required to take up for Bridlington.
s Stops on Saturdays only.
* 2¼ miles to Flamborough Village, and 3¼ miles to Flamborough Lighthouse or the North Landing.
: Nearly 1 mile to H. & B. (Cannon Street) Station.

For Local Trains

BETWEEN	PAGE
Hull and Beverley	765

***** For other Trains**

BETWEEN	PAGE
Driffield and Bridlington	762
Seamer and Scarborough	760 and below.

SCARBOROUGH, SEAMER, and PICKERING.—North Eastern.

Miles	Up.	Week Days only.					
		mrn	mrn	aft	aft	aft	aft
	Scarborough dep.	6 10	9 3	1 40	4 3	7 4	11 5
3	Seamer	6 17	9 10	1 47	4 10	7 11	1111
6¼	Forge Valley	6 25	9 18	1 55	4 18	7 19	1119
8	Wykeham	6 29	9 22	1 59	4 22	7 23	
9¾	Sawdon	6 33	9 26	2 3	4 26	7 27	
11¾	Snainton	6 38	9 31	2 8	4 31	7 32	
14	Ebberston	6 43	9 36	2 13	4 36	7 37	
16¾	Thornton Dale 765	6 49	9 42	2 19	4 42	7 43	
19¼	Pickering 762 arr.	6 56	9 49	2 26	4 49	7 50	

Miles	Down.	Week Days only.				
		mrn	mrn	aft	aft	aft
	Pickering dep.	7 20	1035	2 50	5 29	8 20
3	Thornton Dale	7 27	1042	2 57	5 36	8 27
5½	Ebberston	7 33	1048	3 3	5 42	8 33
8¼	Snainton	7 38	1053	3 8	5 47	8 38
10	Sawdon	7 42	1057	3 12	5 51	8 42
11½	Wykeham	7 47	11 2	3 17	5 56	8 47
13¼	Forge Valley	7 51	11 6	3 21	6 0	8 51
16½	Seamer 760	7 58	1113	3 28	6 7	8 58
19¼	Scarbro' 760 arr.	8 7	1122	3 36	6 15	9 7

For **OTHER TRAINS** between Scarborough and Seamer, see page 760 and above.

A 1914 Timetable

G5 No. 67280 pauses at Cottingham with a local service to Hull.
Photo. K Hoole Collection

1930

This year is included as it marks the beginning of happy developments on the LNER, which the old North Eastern had become, already fortified with the Gresley 'Pacifics' and K 2-6-0s, and with the promise of more to come in the race for express traffic to and from Scotland. On the Bridlington line matters had not yet reached fever pitch, though the timetable looked quite promising. There were eight trains between Hull and Scarborough, three of them stopping everywhere and taking up to 2 ¼ hours for the work. The best runner was the 8.25am. from Scarborough which reached Hull at 9.39, calling only at Filey and Bridlington for two minutes. The return journey was the 5.08pm. which stopped only at the same two places with a 'picks up on request' stop at Beverley, to reach the seaside at 6.29pm. These trains both gave Bridlington commuters a 40-43 min.

run each way. There were other trains of varied grandeur between Hull and Bridlington only, the tried and tested 8am. running non-stop to Hull in 40 min. and back from Hull at 5.30pm. with a 'sets down only' note for Driffield. Was a passenger ever prevented from actually joining these trains I wonder? Manchester Piccadilly has such a restriction for Stockport on London expresses which call there to take up, presumably to stop these trains being choked up with local travellers when other services are available to carry them. Not quite the same scenario as Driffield here, though the principal is, and just as difficult to follow up.

The little gem in 1930 was to be found in the presence of one of the new Sentinel steam railcars which performed the following feat:

Hull dep:	5.10am.
Bridlington arr:	6.10 (non-stop)
Bridlington dep:	6.25am.
Hull arr:	7.30 (calls at Cott. and Bev.)

A G5 0•4•4T waits to leave Beverley on a return push-pull working to Hull.
Photo. C T Goode

A8 4•6•2T No. 69890 gets away from Beverley on a Bridlington train. The van next to the engine will travel all the way. *Photo. C T Goode*

This was probably put on to let Bridlington shed see what the new Hull upstart could do! It was quite an early start for the driver, though.

One other point of interest was a Saturday Only train which left Bridlington at 1.55pm. for Liverpool Cen., probably with only a change of engine and crew at Sheffield, and arriving there at 6.35pm. No journey in the other direction is shown. One late service left Scarborough at 11.15pm SO for Gristhorpe and Filey, when it seems to vanish as no further movement is shown.

The Sunday statutory stoppers still survived, at 7am. from Hull and 5.17pm from Scarborough, along with later, faster ones out and back.

An ex GN class J2. 0•6•0 No.3071 relaxes at Bridlington after bringing up a day excursion, probably from the Bradford area Photo. C T Goode

1939

Moving on to 1939, there were six or seven stopping or semi-fast trains between Hull and Scarborough, the best being the 5.08pm. from Hull, as in 1930 which stopped at Beverley, Driffield SO, Bridlington and Filey, taking 1hr. 28min. Trains to Bridlington were seven, with eleven in the other direction, to Hull. There were now two Up 'Flyers', the 8.05am., arriving Hull at 8.44 non-stop, and the 8.15am. calling at Driffield and Beverley and arriving at 9am. If you managed to miss both of these, then the 8.59am. would see you there at 9.38am., also non-stop. To get the commuters home there was still the 5.30pm., arriving in Bridlington at 6.13pm., with a halt at Driffield. The tradition of this train, hauled by a Bridlington D20 to the end of the shed's life, lasted until 1958. There were three Sunday trains each way.

1942

During the war period the railways managed, on paper at least, to provide a neat and acceptable timetable, with 37-39

HULL, BEVERLEY, DRIFFIELD, BRIDLINGTON, FILEY, and SCARBOROUGH.

Down. — Week Days.

Miles	Down.	mrn	mrn	mrn	mrn	mrn		mrn	mrn	aft	aft	aft	aft	aft	aft
		One class only.						Saturdays only.	Saturdays only.	Saturdays only.	Saturdays only.			Saturdays only. Except 30th inst.	Saturdays only.
	Hull (Paragon) dep.	5 10	5 45	8 0	9 5	1045	..		11 5	1230	1250	1 0	2 15	2 53	3 0
4	Cottingham		5 53	8 8	9 13	1053	..		11 13	1238	..	1 8	2 23		3 8
8¼	Beverley		6 5	8 15	9 22	11 1	..		11 22	1247	Dd	1 17	2 31		3 17
11¼	Arram		..	8 24	..	..	..		11 28		..	1 23	..		
13	Lockington		6 14	8 30	..	..	..		11 33		..	1 28	..		
16¼	Hutton Cranswick		6 21	8 33	..	..	..		11 40		..	1 35	..		
19½	**Driffield 938, 939** arr.		6 27	8 44	9 37	..	..		11 46		1 21	1 41	2 46		
	Driffield dep.		6 31	8 46	9 39	..	..		11 48		1 24	1 46	2 47		
21½	Nafferton		6 36	8 51	..	..	..		11 53		..	1 51	..		
23¾	Lowthorpe		6 41	8 56	..	..	..		11 58		..	1 56	..		
25¼	Burton Agnes		6 46	9 1	..	..	..		12 3		..	2 1	..		
28½	Carnaby		6 52	9 7	..	..	..		12 9		..	2 7	..		
30¾	**Bridlington** arr.	6 10	6 57	9 13	9 55	1130	..		12 14	1 23	1 41	2 12	3 2	3 36	3 48
	Bridlington dep.	..	7 2	9 18	9 59	..	..	1135	12 18	..	1 53	2 17	..		3 55
33¼	Flamborough A	..	7 9	9 25	..	..	..	..	12 25	..	2 2	2 26	..		..
34½	Bempton	..	7 14	9 30	..	..	..	..	12 30	..	..	2 31	..		..
37¼	Speeton	..	7 22	..	..	..	..	..	12 38	..	..	2 39	..		..
41½	Hunmanby	..	7 31	9 45	..	..	..	1157	12 47	..	..	2 47	..		..
44¼	**Filey** arr.	..	7 36	9 50	1019	..	..	12 2	12 52	..	2 18	2 52	..		4 19
	Filey dep.	..	7 38	9 52	1021	..	..	12 5	12 54	..	2 21	2 54	..		4 22
46¼	Gristhorpe	..	7 43	9 57	..	..	..	..	..	..	..	2 59	..		..
48	Cayton	..	7 47	10 1	..	..	..	..	..	..	..	3 3	..	..	..
50¾	Seamer 943, 944	..	7 52	1010	1032	..	..	1218	1 6	..	..	3 9	..	..	4 37
53¾	**Scarborough** (C.) 944 arr.	..	8 0	1015	1038	..	..	1224	1 12	..	2 38	3 15	..	..	4 43
95¾	943 York arr.	..	9 4	1128	1150	..	..	1 42	2 30	..	3 43	4 22	..	..	..

Down. — Week Days (continued) and Sundays.

Down.	aft		aft	aft	aft	aft	aft	aft	aft	aft	aft	Sun. mrn	Sun. mrn	Sun. mrn	Sun. aft
					Except Saturdays.						Thursdays and Saturdays.				
Hull (Paragon) dep.	3 15	..	4 25	5 8	5 30	..	6 5	7 5	7 15	9 15	10 50	7 0	8 0	1025	..
Cottingham	..	..	4 33	..	..	..	6 13	..	7 23	9 23	10A58	7 8	8 8	1033	..
Beverley	3 29	..	4 42	5A21	..	..	6 22	7 19	7 32	9 32	11A6	7 18	8 16	1041	..
Arram	..	..	4 48	..	..	..	..	..	7 38	9 38	..	7 24	8 22	1047	..
Lockington	..	..	4 53	..	..	..	..	..	7 43	S	..	7 29	8 27	1052	..
Hutton Cranswick	..	..	5 0	..	..	..	6 35	..	7 50	S	..	7 36	8 34	..	..
Driffield 938, 939 arr.	3 44	..	5 6	..	5B57	..	6 42	..	7 56	9 50	11B21	7 42	8 40	11 3	..
Driffield dep.	3 46	..	5 8	..	..	..	6 44	..	7 58	9 52	..	7 45	..	11 5	..
Nafferton	..	..	5 13	..	..	..	..	..	8 3	S	..	7 50	..	..	..
Lowthorpe	..	..	5 18	..	..	..	..	..	8 8	S	..	7 55	..	..	..
Burton Agnes	..	..	5 23	..	..	..	..	..	8 13	S	..	8 0	..	..	..
Carnaby	..	..	5 29	..	..	..	..	..	8 19	..	..	8 6	..	..	..
Bridlington arr.	4 2	..	5 34	5 51	6 13	..	7 0	7 49	8 24	10U8	11 39	8 11	..	1121	..
Bridlington dep.	4 6	..	..	5 53		6 20	..	7 51	..	..		8 16	..	1126	7 0
Flamborough A	4 13	..	..	..		6 27	..	7 58	..	..		8 24	..	1134	7 8
Bempton	..	..	..	..		6 32	..	Aa	..	..		8 29	..	..	..
Speeton	..	..	..	..		6 40	..	..	..	..		8 37	..	..	..
Hunmanby	4 29	..	..	..		6 49	..	8 13	..	..		8 46	..	..	..
Filey arr.	4 34	..	..	6 13		6 54	..	8 18	..	..		8 51	..	1152	7 26
Filey dep.	4 36	..	..	6 15		6 56	..	8 20	..	..		8 54	..	1154	7 28
Gristhorpe	..	..	..	..		7 1	..	..	..	..		8 59	..	..	..
Cayton	..	..	..	..		..	..	..	..	..		..	..	..	..
Seamer 943, 944	4 47	..	..	..		7 10	..	..	..	..		9 10	..	..	..
Scarborough (C.) 944 arr.	4 52	..	..	6 29		7 16	..	8 34	..	..		9 15	..	12 9	7 43
943 York arr.	5 50	..	..	..	..	8 47	..	10S55	..	..		12 0	..	8 29	8 44

Up. — Week Days.

Miles	Up.	mrn	mrn	mrn	mrn	mrn	mrn	mrn	mrn	mrn	aft	aft	aft	S	aft
		One class only.									Except Saturdays.	Saturdays only.	Saturdays only.		
	942 York dep.	..	..	..	..	4 55	..	..	9 0	10 0	..	..	..	1250	1255
—	**Scarborough** (Central) dep.		..	..	..	7 38	8 25	..	10 0	1110				2 10	2 25
3	Seamer		..	..	..	7 44	..	..	10 6	1117				2 17	2 32
5¼	Cayton		..	..	..	7 50	..	..	..	1123				..	2 38
7½	Gristhorpe		..	..	..	7 54	..	..	..	1127				..	2 42
9½	**Filey** arr.		..	..	..	7 59	..	..	1016	1132				2 28	2 47
	Filey dep.		..	..	..	8 2	8 39	..	1017	1133				2 31	2 50
12¼	Hunmanby		..	..	..	8 10	..	..	..	1140				2 37	2 57
16½	Speeton		..	..	..	8 19	..	..	..	1149				2 45	3 6
19¼	Bempton		..	..	..	8 25	..	..	..	1155				2 51	3 12
20½	Flamborough A		..	..	..	8 29	..	..	..	1159				2 56	3 16
23	**Bridlington** arr.		..	..	..	8 33	8 59	..	1037	12 3				3 1	3 20
	Bridlington dep.	6 25	6 55	8 0	8 10	..	9 1	9 15	1040	12 8	1 40	1 55	2 20	3 7	..
25¼	Carnaby	..	7 0	..	..	..	..	..	1045	1213	..	..	..	..	..
28¼	Burton Agnes	..	7 7	..	..	..	..	..	1051	1219	1 49	..	..	..	..
30	Lowthorpe	..	7 12	..	..	..	..	..	1056	1224	1 54	..	..	..	..
32¼	Nafferton	..	7 17	..	..	..	..	..	11 1	1229	1 59	..	..	3 21	..
34¼	**Driffield 938, 939** arr.	..	7 22	..	8 27	..	..	9 31	11 6	1234	2 4	..	2 36	3 26	..
	Driffield dep.	..	7 24	..	8 29	..	..	9 32	11 8	1237	2 6	..	2 38	3 28	..
37¼	Hutton Cranswick	..	7 32	..	..	..	..	9 39	..	1244	..	..	..	3 35	..
40¾	Lockington	..	7 40	..	..	..	..	..	..	1251	..	..	..	3 42	..
42¼	Arram	..	7 47	..	..	..	..	9 48	..	1256	..	..	..	3 47	..
45¼	Beverley 938	7 15	7 55	..	8B44	..	..	9 55	1125	1 5	2 23	..	2 55	3 55	..
49¾	Cottingham [936	7 22	8 3	..	..	..	..	10 2	..	1 12	2 30	..	3 2	4 3	..
53¾	**Hull** B 932, 932a, 933, arr.	7 30	8 11	8 40	8 59	..	9 39	1010	1138	1 20	2 38	..	3 10	4 12	..

Through Express, Bridlington to Liverpool (Cen.) arr. 6 35 aft., see pages 932 and 913.

Up. — Week Days (continued) and Sundays.

Up.	aft	aft	aft	aft	aft	aft	aft	E	S	aft	aft	aft	Sun. mrn	Sun. mrn	Sun. aft	Sun. aft
							Thursdays only.			Saturdays only.		Saturdays only.				
942 York dep.	..	2 43	3 40	4 55	5 30	..		7 5	7 5	8 15	..	8 15	..	10 5	..	6 0
Scarborough (Central) dep.	..	4 15	5 10	6 7	6 30	..		8 25	8 25	9 45	..	11 5	..	1120	5 17	8 5
Seamer	..	..	5 16	..	6 36	..		8 31	8 31	..	..	1111	..	..	5 23	..
Cayton	..	..	5 22	..	..	..		..	..	..	..	..	..	..	..	..
Gristhorpe	..	..	5 26	6 18	6 43	..		..	..	..	..	1119	..	..	5 33	..
Filey arr.	..	4 29	5 31	6 23	6 48	..		8 41	8 41	10 0	..	1124	..	1134	5 38	8 19
Filey dep.	..	4 32	5 32	6 26	6 51	..		8 42	8 42	10 2	..		..	1136	5 40	8 20
Hunmanby	..	..	5 40	..	..	..		8 49	8 49	..	..		..	..	5 47	..
Speeton	..	..	5 49	..	..	..		..	..	..	..		..	..	5 57	..
Bempton	..	..	5 55	..	..	..		..	..	..	..		..	..	6 3	..
Flamborough A	..	..	6 0	6 46	7 11	..		9 6	9 6	..	..		..	1156	6 8	..
Bridlington arr.	..	4 54	6 4	6 51	7 15	..		9 10	9 10	1024	..		..	12 0	6 12	8 42
Bridlington dep.	3 30	5 0	6 9	6 55	7 20	8 20	8 30	9 12	9 14		1030		..	..	6 21	8 50
Carnaby	3 35	..	6 14	..	..	..	8 35	..	9 19		..		..	..	6 26	..
Burton Agnes	3 41	5 9	6 20	..	..	..	8 41	..	9 25		..		..	..	6 32	..
Lowthorpe	3 46	5 14	6 25	..	..	..	8 46	..	9 30		..		..	..	6 37	..
Nafferton	3 51	5 19	6 30	..	..	..	8 51	..	9 35		S		..	..	6 42	..
Driffield 938, 939 arr.	3 56	5 24	6 35	7 11	7 36	8 36	8 56	9 28	9 40		1046		..	..	6 47	9 6
Driffield dep.	3 58	5 27	6 38	7 13	7 38	8 38	8 58	9 29	9 41		1048		8 51	..	6 48	9 7
Hutton Cranswick	4 5	..	6 45	..	..	..	9 5	..	9 48		..		8 59	..	6 55	..
Lockington	4 12	..	6 52	..	..	..	9 12	..	9 54		..		9 7	..	7 2	..
Arram	4 17	..	6 57	..	..	..	9 17	..	10 0		..		9 13	..	7 7	..
Beverley 938	4 25	5 45	7 5	7 30	7 55	8 55	9 25	9 45	1010		11 5		9 21	..	7 15	9 25
Cottingham [936	4 32	5 52	7 13	7 37	8 2	..	9 32	9 52	1017		..		[illegible]	..	[illegible]	[illegible]
Hull B 932, 932a, 933, arr.	4 40	6 0	7 21	7 45	[illegible]	[illegible]	9 40	[illegible]	[illegible]		[illegible]		[illegible]	[illegible]	[illegible]	[illegible]

A 2½ miles to Flamborough Village, and 3¼ miles to Flamborough Lighthouse o[illegible] North Landing [illegible] when required to set down. [illegible] B Paragon [illegible]

Timetable from the1930.

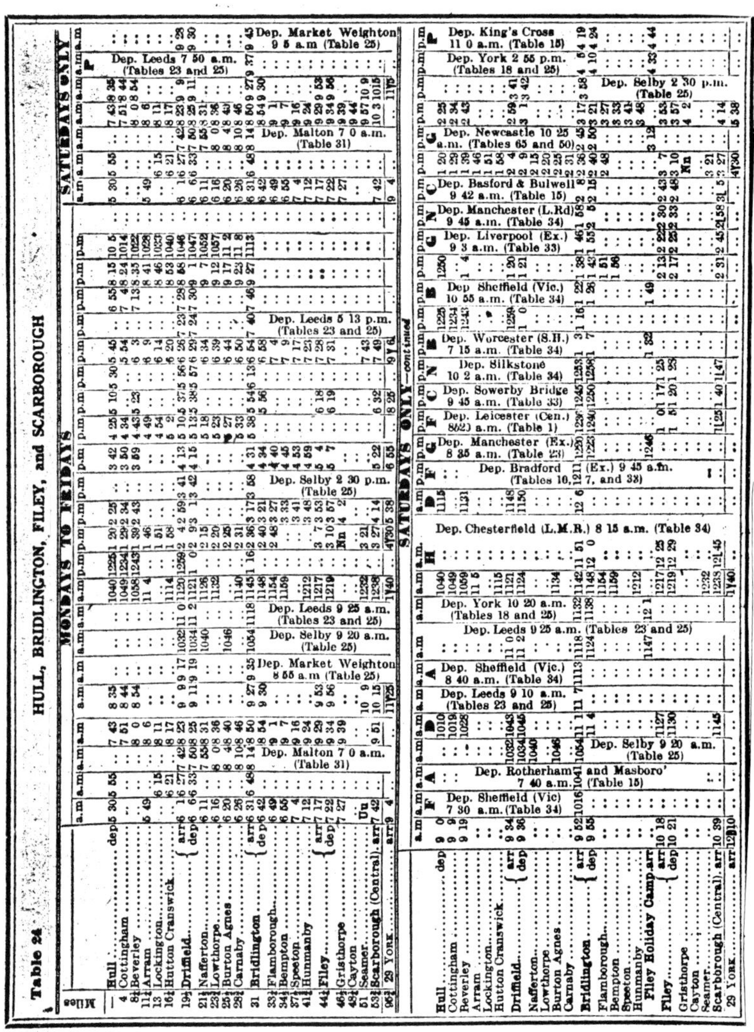

Table 24 — HULL, BRIDLINGTON, FILEY, and SCARBOROUGH

MONDAYS TO FRIDAYS

Miles	Station	a.m	a.m	a.m Dep. Malton 7 0 a.m. (Table 31)	a.m	a.m	a.m Dep. Market Weighton 8 55 a.m (Table 25)	a.m Dep. Selby 9 20 a.m. (Table 25)	a.m Dep. Leeds 9 25 a.m. (Tables 23 and 25)
—	Hull dep	5 30	5 55	..	7 43	8 35	..	..	..
4	Cottingham	..	..	..	7 51	8 44	..	..	..
8½	Beverley	..	..	..	8 0	8 54	..	..	..
11½	Arram	5 49	..	..	8 6	..	..	..	..
13	Lockington	..	6 15	..	8 11	..	..	..	..
16½	Hutton Cranswick	..	6 21	..	8 17	..	..	..	..
19½	Driffield arr	6 1	6 27	7 42	8 23	9 9	9 17	1032	11 0
	Driffield dep	6 6	6 33	7 50	8 25	9 11	9 19	1034	11 2
21½	Nafferton	6 11	..	7 55	8 31	..	..	1040	..
23½	Lowthorpe	6 16	..	8 0	8 36	..	..	..	..
25½	Burton Agnes	6 20	..	8 4	8 40	..	..	1046	..
28½	Carnaby	6 26	..	8 10	8 46	..	..	..	..
31	Bridlington arr	6 31	6 48	8 14	8 50	9 27	9 35	1054	1118
	Bridlington dep	6 42	..		8 54	9 30			
33½	Flamborough	6 49	..		9 1	..			
34½	Bempton	6 55	..		9 7	..			
37½	Speeton	7 4	..		9 16	..			
41½	Hunmanby	7 12	..		9 24	..			
44½	Filey arr	7 17	..		9 29	9 53			
	Filey dep	7 22	..		9 34	9 56			
46½	Gristhorpe	7 27	..		9 39	..			
48½	Cayton	..	..		..	..			
51	Seamer	Uu	..		..	10 9			
53½	Scarborough (Central) arr	7 42	..		9 51	10 15			
96½	29 York arr	9 4	..		..	11Y25			

Miles	Station	a.m	p.m	p.m	p.m	p.m Dep. Selby 2 30 p.m. (Table 25)	p.m	p.m	p.m
—	Hull dep	1040	1225	1 20	2 25	..	3 42	4 25	5 10
4	Cottingham	1049	1234	1 29	2 34	..	3 50	4 34	..
8½	Beverley	1058	1243	1 39	2 43	..	3 59	4 43	5 23
11½	Arram	11 4	..	1 46	..	..	..	4 49	..
13	Lockington	..	..	1 51	..	..	..	4 54	..
16½	Hutton Cranswick	1114	..	1 58	..	..	..	5 2	..
19½	Driffield arr	1120	1259	2 4	2 59	3 41	4 13	5 10	5 37
	Driffield dep	1121	1 0	2 9	3 1	3 42	4 15	5 13	5 38
21½	Nafferton	1126	..	2 15	..	..	..	5 18	..
23½	Lowthorpe	1132	..	2 20	..	..	..	5 23	..
25½	Burton Agnes	..	..	2 25	..	..	..	5 27	..
28½	Carnaby	1140	..	2 31	..	..	..	5 33	..
31	Bridlington arr	1145	1 16	2 36	3 17	3 58	4 31	5 38	5 54
	Bridlington dep	1148	..	2 40	3 21		4 34	..	5 56
33½	Flamborough	1154	..	2 48	3 27		4 40	..	..
34½	Bempton	1159	..	..	3 33		4 45	..	..
37½	Speeton	..	..	..	3 41		4 53	..	..
41½	Hunmanby	1212	..	..	3 48		4 59	..	..
44½	Filey arr	1217	..	3 7	3 53		5 4	..	6 18
	Filey dep	1219	..	3 10	3 57		5 7	..	6 19
46½	Gristhorpe	..	..	Nn	4 2		..	..	..
48½	Cayton	..	..	..	..		..	..	..
51	Seamer	1232	..	3 21	..		..	..	..
53½	Scarborough (Central) arr	1238	..	3 27	4 14		5 22	..	6 32
96½	29 York arr	1Y40	..	4Y30	5 38		6 55	..	8 25

Miles	Station	p.m	p.m	p.m Dep. Leeds 5 13 p.m. (Tables 23 and 25)	p.m	p.m	p.m	
—	Hull dep	5 30	5 45	..	6 55	8 15	10 5	..
4	Cottingham	..	5 54	..	7 4	8 24	1014	..
8½	Beverley	..	6 3	..	7 13	8 35	1022	..
11½	Arram	..	6 9	..	..	8 41	1028	..
13	Lockington	..	6 14	..	..	8 46	1033	..
16½	Hutton Cranswick	..	6 20	..	..	8 53	1040	..
19½	Driffield arr	5 56	6 26	7 23	7 28	8 58	1046	..
	Driffield dep	5 57	6 29	7 24	7 30	9 1	1047	..
21½	Nafferton	..	6 34	..	..	9 7	1052	..
23½	Lowthorpe	..	6 39	..	..	9 12	1057	..
25½	Burton Agnes	..	6 44	..	..	9 17	11 2	..
28½	Carnaby	..	6 50	..	..	9 23	11 8	..
31	Bridlington arr	6 13	6 54	7 40	7 46	9 27	1113	..
	Bridlington dep	..	6 58		..	..	..	..
33½	Flamborough	..	7 4		..	..	..	..
34½	Bempton	..	7 9		..	..	..	..
37½	Speeton	..	7 17		..	..	..	..
41½	Hunmanby	..	7 23		..	..	..	..
44½	Filey arr	..	7 28		..	..	..	..
	Filey dep	..	7 31		..	..	..	..
46½	Gristhorpe	..	..		..	..	..	..
48½	Cayton	..	..		..	..	..	..
51	Seamer	..	7 43		..	..	..	..
53½	Scarborough (Central) arr	..	7 49		..	..	..	..
96½	29 York arr	..	9Y6		..	..	..	..

SATURDAYS ONLY

Miles	Station	a.m	a.m	a.m Dep. Malton 7 0 a.m. (Table 31)	a.m	a.m	a.m P Dep. Leeds 7 50 a.m. (Tables 23 and 25)	a.m Dep. Market Weighton 9 5 a.m (Table 25)
—	Hull dep	5 30	5 55	..	7 43	8 35		..
4	Cottingham	..	..	..	7 51	8 44		..
8½	Beverley	..	..	..	8 0	8 54		..
11½	Arram	5 49	..	..	8 6	..		..
13	Lockington	..	6 15	..	8 11	..		..
16½	Hutton Cranswick	..	6 21	..	8 17	..		..
19½	Driffield arr	6 1	6 27	7 42	8 23	9 9		9 28
	Driffield dep	6 6	6 33	7 50	8 25	9 11		9 30
21½	Nafferton	6 11	..	7 55	8 31	..		..
23½	Lowthorpe	6 16	..	8 0	8 36	..		..
25½	Burton Agnes	6 20	..	8 4	8 40	..		..
28½	Carnaby	6 26	..	8 10	8 46	..		..
31	Bridlington arr	6 31	6 48	8 14	8 50	9 27	9 37	9 45
	Bridlington dep	6 42	..		8 54	9 30	..	
33½	Flamborough	6 49	..		9 1	..	..	
34½	Bempton	6 55	..		9 7	..	..	
37½	Speeton	7 4	..		9 16	..	..	
41½	Hunmanby	7 12	..		9 24	..	..	
44½	Filey arr	7 17	..		9 29	9 53	..	
	Filey dep	7 22	..		9 34	9 56	..	
46½	Gristhorpe	7 27	..		9 39	..	..	
48½	Cayton	..	..		9 44	..	..	
51	Seamer	..	..		9 57	10 9	..	
53½	Scarborough (Central) arr	7 42	..		10 3	1015	..	
96½	29 York arr	9 4	..		..	11Y5	..	

SATURDAYS ONLY—continued

Station	a.m	a.m F Dep. Sheffield (Vic) 7 30 a.m. (Table 34)	a.m A Dep. Rotherham and Masboro' 7 40 a.m. (Table 15)	a.m Dep. Selby 9 20 a.m. (Table 25)	a.m D	a.m Dep. Leeds 9 10 a.m. (Tables 23 and 25)	a.m A Dep. Sheffield (Vic.) 8 40 a.m. (Table 34)	a.m Dep. Leeds 9 25 a.m. (Tables 23 and 25)
Hull dep	9 0		..	..	1010			..
Cottingham	9 9		..	..	1019			..
Beverley	9 19			..	1028			..
Arram	..			..	..			..
Lockington	..			..	..			..
Hutton Cranswick	..			..	..			..
Driffield arr	9 34			1032	1043			11 0
Driffield dep	9 36			1034	1045			11 2
Nafferton	..			1040	..			..
Lowthorpe	..			..	..			..
Burton Agnes	..			1046	..			..
Carnaby	..			..	..			..
Bridlington arr	9 52	1016	1041	1054	11 1	11 7	1113	1118
Bridlington dep	9 55	..			11 4	..	..	1124
Flamborough	..	..			..	..	..	..
Bempton	..	..			..	..	..	..
Speeton	..	..			..	..	..	..
Hunmanby	..	..			..	..	..	..
Filey Holiday Camp arr	..	..			..	..	..	1147
Filey arr	10 18	..			1127	..	..	..
Filey dep	10 21	..			1130	..	..	..
Gristhorpe	..	..			..	..	..	..
Cayton	..	..			..	..	..	..
Seamer	..	..	..		..	..	..	..
Scarborough (Central) arr	10 39	..	..		1145	..	..	..
29 York arr	12 10	..	..	..	..	..	..	..

Station	a.m Dep. York 10 20 a.m. (Tables 18 and 25)	a.m	a.m. H	Dep. Chesterfield (L.M.R.) 8 15 a.m. (Table 34)	a.m D	p.m F Dep. Bradford (Ex.) 9 45 a.m. (Tables 10, 7, and 33)	p.m G Dep. Manchester (Ex.) 8 35 a.m. (Table 23)	p.m F Dep. Leicester (Cen.) 8?2 a.m. (Table 1)
Hull dep		1040	..		1115	..		
Cottingham		1049	..		..	..		
Beverley		1059	..		1131			
Arram		11 5	..		..			
Lockington		..	..		..			
Hutton Cranswick		1115	..		..			
Driffield arr		1121	..		1148			
Driffield dep		1124	..		1150			
Nafferton		..	..		..			
Lowthorpe		..	..		..			
Burton Agnes		1134	..		..			
Carnaby		..	..		..			
Bridlington arr	1132	1142	11 51		12 6	1211	1220	1236
Bridlington dep	1138	1148	12 0		..		1223	1240
Flamborough	..	1154	..		..		..	..
Bempton	..	1159	..		..		..	..
Speeton	..	..	..		..		..	..
Hunmanby	..	1212	..		..		..	..
Filey Holiday Camp arr	12 1	..	..		..		1246	..
Filey arr	..	1217	12 25		..		..	1 0
Filey dep	..	1219	12 29		..		..	1 5
Gristhorpe	..	..	..		..	..	..	..
Cayton	..	..	..		..	..	..	..
Seamer	..	1232	..		..	..	..	..
Scarborough (Central) arr	..	1238	12L45		..	..	..	1L25
29 York arr	..	1Y40	..		..	..	..	..

Station	p.m C Dep. Sowerby Bridge 9 45 a.m. (Table 33)	p.m N Dep. Silkstone 10 2 a.m. (Table 34)	p.m B Dep. Worcester (S.H.) 7 15 a.m. (Table 34)	p.m	p.m B Dep Sheffield (Vic.) 10 55 a.m. (Table 34)	p.m	p.m G Dep. Liverpool (Ex.) 9 3 a.m. (Table 33)	p.m N Dep. Manchester (L.Rd) 9 45 a.m. (Table 34)
Hull dep				1225		1250		
Cottingham				1234		..		
Beverley				1243		1 4		
Arram				..		..		
Lockington				..		..		
Hutton Cranswick				..		..		
Driffield arr				1259		1 20		
Driffield dep				1 0		1 21		
Nafferton				..		..		
Lowthorpe				..		..		
Burton Agnes				..		..		
Carnaby				..		..		
Bridlington arr	1245	1253	1 3	1 16	1 22	1 38	1 46	1 58
Bridlington dep	1250	1258	1 7	..	1 26	1 43	1 55	2 5
Flamborough	..	..	..	..	..	1 51	..	..
Bempton	..	..	..	..	..	1 56	..	..
Speeton	..	..	..	..	..	..	..	..
Hunmanby	..	..	..	..	..	..	..	..
Filey Holiday Camp arr	..	..	1 32	..	1 49	..	..	..
Filey arr	1 17	1 25	..	..	..	2 13	2 22	2 30
Filey dep	1 20	1 28	..	..	..	2 17	2 25	2 33
Gristhorpe	..	..	..	..	..	..	..	..
Cayton	..	..	..	..	..	..	..	..
Seamer	..	..	..	..	..	..	..	..
Scarborough (Central) arr	1 40	1L47	..	..	..	2 31	2 45	2L58
29 York arr	..	..	..	..	..	..	..	..

Station	p.m C Dep. Basford & Bulwell 9 42 a.m. (Table 15)	p.m	p.m G Dep. Newcastle 10 25 a.m. (Tables 65 and 50)	p.m	p.m Dep. Selby 2 30 p.m. (Table 25)	p.m Dep. York 2 55 p.m. (Tables 18 and 25)	p.m P Dep. King's Cross 11 0 a.m. (Table 15)
Hull dep		1 20		2 25	..		
Cottingham		1 29		2 34	..		
Beverley		1 39		2 43	..		
Arram		1 46		..	..		
Lockington		1 51		..	..		
Hutton Cranswick		1 58		..	..		
Driffield arr		2 4		2 59	3 41		
Driffield dep		2 9		3 1	3 42		
Nafferton		2 15		..	..		
Lowthorpe		2 20		..	..		
Burton Agnes		2 25		..	..		
Carnaby		2 31		..	..		
Bridlington arr	2 8	2 36	2 45	3 17	3 58	4 5	4 19
Bridlington dep	2 15	2 40	2 50	3 21		4 10	4 24
Flamborough	..	2 48	..	3 27		..	..
Bempton	..	..	..	3 33		..	..
Speeton	..	..	..	3 41		..	..
Hunmanby	..	..	..	3 48		..	..
Filey Holiday Camp arr	..	..	3 12	..		4 33	4 44
Filey arr	2 43	3 7	..	3 53		..	..
Filey dep	2 48	3 10	..	3 57		..	..
Gristhorpe	..	Nn	..	4 2		..	..
Cayton	..	..	..	..		..	..
Seamer	..	3 21	..	..		..	..
Scarborough (Central) arr	3L 5	3 27	..	4 14		..	..
29 York arr	..	4Y30	..	5 38		..	..

1939 Timetable

Right: A timetable from 1942

Table 105 — HULL, BRIDLINGTON, FILEY, and SCARBOROUGH

Week Days

Miles	Station		mrn	mrn	mrn		mrn	mrn	mrn	mrn	
—	Hull	dep	5 38	5 50	..	..	8 0	9 5	..	11 5	..
4	Cottingham		..	5 58	..	..	8 8	9 13	..	1113	..
8¼	Beverley		..	6 10	..	..	8 17	9 22	..	1125	..
11½	Arram		..	..	..	..	8 25	..	..	1131	..
13	Lockington		..	6 19	..	..	8 30	..	..	..	..
16¼	Hutton Cranswick		..	6 25	..	..	8 36	..	..	1140	..
19½	Driffield	arr	6 4	6 31	..	..	8 42	9 37	1042	1146	..
		dep	6 7	6 33	8 0	..	8 46	9 39	1043	1148	..
21½	Nafferton		..	6 40	8 5	..	8 51	..	1049	1153	..
23¾	Lowthorpe		..	6 43	8 10	..	8 56	..	..	1158	..
25½	Burton Agnes		..	6 49	8 14	..	9 0	..	1055	Aa	..
28½	Carnaby		..	6 55	8 20	..	9 6	..	..	Aa	..
30½	Bridlington	arr	6 22	6 59	8 24	..	9 10	9 55	11 5	12 8	..
		dep	..	7 2	..	..	..	9 57	Dep. Selby 9 30 mrn (Table 106)	1212	..
33¼	Flamborough		..	7 8	..	..	..	..		1218	..
34½	Bempton		..	7 13	..	..	..	..		1223	..
37½	Speeton		..	7 21	..	..	..	..		1231	..
41½	Hunmanby		..	7 28	..	..	..	..		1238	..
44¼	Filey	arr	..	7 33	..	..	..	1019		1243	..
		dep	..	7 37	..	..	..	1020		1245	..
46½	Gristhorpe		..	7 42	..	..	..	..		..	..
48¾	Cayton		..	Ss	..	..	..	..		..	..
50¾	Seamer		..	Nn	..	..	..	1031		1255	..
53¾	Scarborough (Central)	arr	..	7 56	..	..	..	1037		1 1	..
95½	109 York	arr	..	9 9	..	..	..	11Y40		2Y7	..

Station		aft E	aft S	aft	aft S	aft	aft	aft	aft E	
Hull	dep	..	1250	1 20	..	2 55	..	4 30	5 20	..
Cottingham		..	..	1 28	..	3 3	..	4 38	..	..
Beverley		..	1 4	1 38	..	3 11	..	4 46	5 34	..
Arram		..	..	1 45	..	..	..	4 52	..	..
Lockington		..	..	1 50	..	..	..	4 57	..	..
Hutton Cranswick		..	..	1 57	..	..	..	5 3	..	..
Driffield	arr	..	1 20	2 3	..	3 27	3 48	5 13	5 49	..
	dep	..	1 21	2 8	..	3 28	3 52	5 15	5 50	..
Nafferton		..	..	2 13	..	..	..	5 20	..	..
Lowthorpe		..	..	2 18	..	..	..	5 25	..	..
Burton Agnes		..	..	2 23	..	..	..	5 29	..	..
Carnaby		..	..	2 29	..	..	..	5 35	..	..
Bridlington	arr	..	1 38	2 34	..	3 44	4 9	5 39	6 6	..
	dep	1 43	1 43	..	2 40	3 46	Dep. Selby 2 36 aft (Table 106)	..	6 10	..
Flamborough		1 51	1 51	..	2 48	3 53		..	..	..
Bempton		..	..	..	..	3 58		..	..	..
Speeton		..	..	..	..	4 6		..	..	..
Hunmanby		..	..	..	..	4 13		..	..	..
Filey	arr	2 10	2 10	..	3 7	4 18		..	6 32	..
	dep	2 14	2 14	..	3 10	4 19		..	6 34	..
Gristhorpe		..	..	..	..	4 24		..	..	..
Cayton		..	..	..	—	..		..	..	..
Seamer		..	..	..	..	4 33		..	..	..
Scarborough (Central)	arr	2 28	2 33	..	3 24	4 39		..	6 48	..
109 York	arr	..	..	..	4 44	5Y37		..	..	..

Station		aft	aft	aft		aft					Sundays mrn		Sundays aft	
Hull	dep	5 30	..	7 10	..	9 30	..	—	—	..	7 0	..	6 0	..
Cottingham		5 38	..	7 19	..	9 38	..	—	..	..	7 8	..	6 8	..
Beverley		5 47	..	7 30	..	9 47	..	..	..	..	7 20	..	6 17	..
Arram		5 53	..	7 35	..	9 53	..	..	..	..	7 26	..	..	..
Lockington		5 58	..	7 40	..	9 58	..	..	..	..	7 31	..	..	..
Hutton Cranswick		6 4	..	7 47	..	10 4	..	..	..	..	7 38	..	..	..
Driffield	arr	6 10	7 3	7 52	..	1010	..	..	..	..	7 44	..	6 34	..
	dep	6 14	7 4	7 55	..	..	..	..	..	..	7 47	..	6 37	..
Nafferton		6 19	..	8 0	..	..	..	..	..	..	7 52	..	..	..
Lowthorpe		6 24	..	8 5	..	..	..	..	..	..	7 57	..	..	..
Burton Agnes		6 29	Hh	8 10	..	..	..	..	..	..	8 2	..	..	..
Carnaby		6 35	..	8 16	..	..	..	..	..	..	8 8	..	..	..
Bridlington	arr	6 39	7 26	8 20	..	..	..	..	..	..	8 13	..	6 53	..
	dep	6 44	Dep. Selby 5 48 aft (Table 106)	..	..	..	..	..	..	..	8 16	..	7 1	..
Flamborough		6 50		..	..	..	..	..	..	..	8 22	..	7 8	..
Bempton		6 55		..	..	..	..	..	..	..	8 27	..	7 13	..
Speeton		7 3		..	..	..	..	..	..	..	8 35	..	7 21	..
Hunmanby		7 9		..	..	..	..	..	..	..	8 44	..	7 28	..
Filey	arr	7 14		..	..	..	..	..	..	..	8 49	..	7 33	..
	dep	7 17		..	..	..	..	..	..	..	8 52	..	7 35	..
Gristhorpe		—		..	..	..	..	..	..	..	8 57	..	..	..
Cayton		..		..	..	..	..	..	..	..	..	..	..	..
Seamer		7 29		..	..	..	..	..	..	..	9 8	..	7 46	..
Scarborough (Central)	arr	7 35		..	..	..	..	..	..	..	9 14	..	7 51	..
109 York	arr	9Y7		..	..	..	..	..	..	..	1135	..	8Y48	..

Week Days

Miles	Station		mrn		mrn		mrn	mrn		mrn	mrn
	109 York	dep	..	..	Arr. Selby 8 52 mrn (Table 106)	..	..	..	..	4 35	..
—	Scarborough (Central)	dep	..	..		..	..	..	..	7 30	..
3	Seamer		..	..		..	..	..	..	7 36	..
5¼	Cayton		..	..		..	..	..	..	..	..
7¼	Gristhorpe		..	..		..	..	..	..	7 46	..
9½	Filey	arr	..	..		..	..	..	..	7 51	..
		dep	..	..		..	..	..	..	7 53	..
12¼	Hunmanby		..	..		..	..	..	..	7 59	..
16¼	Speeton		..	..		..	..	..	..	8 7	..
19¼	Bempton		..	..		..	..	..	..	8 13	..
20½	Flamborough		..	..		..	..	..	..	8 16	..
23	Bridlington	arr	..	..		..	..	..	..	8 20	..
		dep	6 30	..	7 15	..	7 20	8 0	..	..	8 35
25¼	Carnaby		..	..	..	..	7 25	..	..	..	8 40
28½	Burton Agnes		..	..	..	..	7 31	..	..	..	..
30	Lowthorpe		..	..	Yy	..	7 35	..	..	..	..
32¼	Nafferton		..	..	7 31	..	7 40	..	..	..	..
34¼	Driffield	arr	6 45	..	7 37	..	7 45	8 14	..	..	8 53
		dep	6 46	..	7 39	..	7 46	8 16	..	..	..
37½	Hutton Cranswick		..	..	..	..	7 53	..	..	..	..
40¾	Lockington		..	..	..	..	8 1	..	..	..	..
42¾	Arram		..	..	..	..	8 8	..	..	..	..
45¼	Beverley		7 1	..	..	..	8 15	8 33	..	..	..
49¾	Cottingham		7 9	..	..	..	8 23	..	..	..	..
53¾	Hull	arr	7 16	..	..	..	8 31	8 47	..	..	..

Station			mrn	mrn	mrn		mrn		aft E	aft S
109 York	dep	..	..	..	..	..	10Y10	..	..	..
Scarborough (Central)	dep	..	8 16	..	..	..	11 15	..	1 7	1 7
Seamer		..	..	..	..	..	11 22	..	1 13	1 13
Cayton		..	..	..	..	—	Ss	..	..	..
Gristhorpe		..	..	..	..	..	Ss	..	..	..
Filey	arr	..	8 30	..	..	..	11 35	..	1 24	1 24
	dep	..	8 31	..	..	..	11 36	..	1 25	1 25
Hunmanby		..	..	..	..	..	11 42	..	..	..
Speeton		..	..	..	..	..	11 50	..	..	..
Bempton		..	..	..	..	..	11 56	..	..	..
Flamborough		..	..	..	..	..	11 59	..	..	..
Bridlington	arr	..	8 52	..	..	..	12 3	..	1 46	1 46
	dep	..	8 54	9 10	1020	..	12 8	..	..	1 51
Carnaby		..	..	..	..	..	12 13	..	..	..
Burton Agnes		..	..	9 19	..	..	12 19	..	..	..
Lowthorpe		..	..	9 23	..	..	12 23	..	..	2 2
Nafferton		..	..	9 29	..	..	12 28	..	..	2 7
Driffield	arr	..	9 9	9 33	1036	..	12 33	..	..	2 12
	dep	..	9 10	9 34	1038	..	12 35	..	..	2 14
Hutton Cranswick		..	..	9 40	..	..	12 41	..	..	..
Lockington		..	..	..	..	..	12 47	..	..	..
Arram		..	..	9 49	..	..	12 52	..	..	..
Beverley		..	9 26	9 56	1055	..	1 2	..	..	2 32
Cottingham		..	..	10 3	11 2	..	1 9	..	..	2 39
Hull	arr	..	9 38	1011	1110	..	1 17	..	..	2 47

Station		aft	aft	aft	aft	aft	aft	aft			Sundays mrn		Sundays aft	
109 York	dep	1SY20		3 0	..		5Y20	..	..	..	4 35	..	9a10	..
Scarborough (Central)	dep	2 25	Arr. Selby 5 0 aft (Table 106)	4 25	..	Arr. Selby 8 14 aft (Table 106)	6 27	..	..	..	10 0	..	6 0	..
Seamer		2 32		Uu	..		6 33	..	..	..	10 7	..	6 7	..
Cayton		..		..	..		..	..	..	..	..	..	..	..
Gristhorpe		..		..	..		6 41	..	..	..	1015	..	6 15	..
Filey	arr	2 43		4 39	..		6 46	..	..	..	1020	..	6 20	..
	dep	2 44		4 41	..		6 48	..	..	..	1022	..	6 22	..
Hunmanby		2 50		..	..		6 53	..	..	..	1028	..	6 29	..
Speeton		2 59		..	..		7 2	..	..	..	1036	..	6 38	..
Bempton		3 5		4 58	..		7 8	..	..	..	1042	..	6 44	..
Flamborough		3 9		..	..		7 15	..	..	..	1045	..	6 48	..
Bridlington	arr	3 13		5 5	..		7 19	..	..	..	1050	..	6 52	..
	dep	3 15	3 30	5 9	6 20	6 58	7 22	..	..	..	1055	..	7 1	..
Carnaby		3 20	..	..	6 25	..	..	..	..	..	11 0	..	7 6	..
Burton Agnes		3 26	..	5 17	6 31	..	..	..	..	..	11 6	..	7 12	..
Lowthorpe		3 31	..	5 21	6 35	..	Zz	..	..	..	1110	..	7 16	..
Nafferton		3 36	..	5 26	6 40	..	Zz	..	..	..	1115	..	7 21	..
Driffield	arr	3 41	3 46	5 31	6 45	7 12	7 38	..	..	..	1120	..	7 28	..
	dep	3 43	3 48	5 33	6 47	7 13	7 40	1028	..	..	1122	..	7 29	..
Hutton Cranswick		3 50	..	..	6 53	..	..	1035	..	..	1129	..	7 36	..
Lockington		3 57	..	..	6 59	..	..	..	..	..	1137	..	7 43	..
Arram		4 2	..	..	7 4	..	..	..	..	..	1145	..	7 48	..
Beverley		4 10	..	5 51	7 12	..	7 58	1048	..	..	1153	..	7 56	..
Cottingham		4 17	..	5 58	7 19	..	8 5	1056	..	..	12 1	..	8 3	..
Hull	arr	4 25	..	6 7	7 29	..	8 13	11 5	..	..	1210	..	8 11	..

Aa Calls on Weds and Sats. *a* Morn. **E** Except Saturdays. **Hh** Calls to set down except on Saturdays. **Nn** Calls on Mons. only.
S Saturdays only. **Ss** Calls on Sats. only. **Uu** Calls on Mondays when required to take up.
Y Connection at Seamer. **Yy** Calls when required to take up only. **Zz** Calls when required to set down only.

For **LOCAL TRAINS** between Hull and Beverley, see Table 97. For **OTHER TRAINS** between Seamer and Scarborough, Tables 109 & 112.

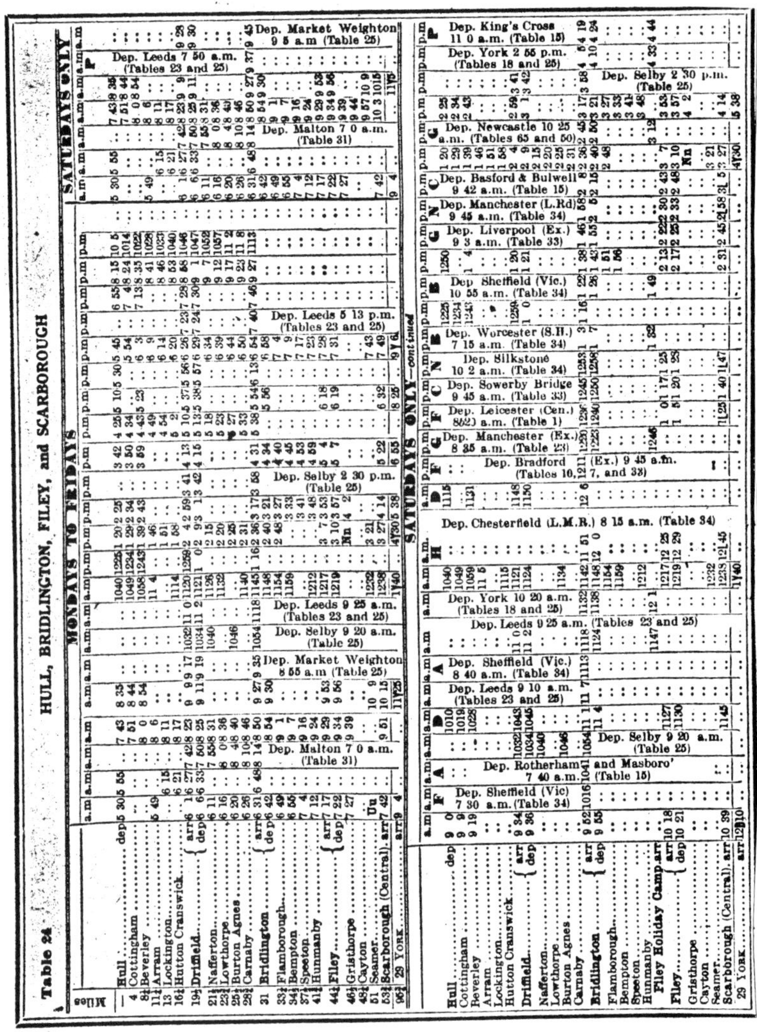

Table 24 — HULL, BRIDLINGTON, FILEY, and SCARBOROUGH

MONDAYS TO FRIDAYS / SATURDAYS ONLY / SATURDAYS ONLY—continued

Miles	Station
—	Hull .... dep
4	Cottingham
8¼	Beverley
11½	Arram
13	Lockington
16½	Hutton Cranswick
19½	Driffield .... arr / dep
21½	Nafferton
23¾	Lowthorpe
25½	Burton Agnes
28½	Carnaby
31	Bridlington .... arr / dep
33¾	Flamborough
34½	Bempton
37½	Speeton
41½	Hunmanby
44½	Filey .... arr / dep
46½	Gristhorpe
48½	Cayton
51	Seamer
53½	Scarborough (Central) .... arr
96½	29 York .... arr

Dep. Market Weighton 8 55 a.m. (Table 25) — Dep. Selby 9 20 a.m. (Table 25) — Dep. Leeds 9 25 a.m. (Tables 23 and 25) — Dep. Malton 7 0 a.m. (Table 31) — Dep. Selby 2 30 p.m. (Table 25) — Dep. Leeds 5 13 p.m. (Tables 23 and 25) — Dep. Leeds 7 50 a.m. (Tables 23 and 25) — Dep. Market Weighton 9 5 a.m. (Table 25)

Dep. Sheffield (Vic) 7 30 a.m. (Table 34) — Dep. Rotherham and Masboro' 7 40 a.m. (Table 15) — Dep. Leeds 9 10 a.m. (Tables 23 and 25) — Dep. Sheffield (Vic.) 8 40 a.m. (Table 34) — Dep. Leeds 9 25 a.m. (Tables 23 and 25) — Dep. York 10 20 a.m. (Tables 18 and 25) — Dep. Chesterfield (L.M.R.) 8 15 a.m. (Table 34) — Dep. Bradford (Ex.) 9 45 a.m. (Tables 10, 17, and 33) — Dep. Manchester (Ex.) 8 35 a.m. (Table 23) — Dep. Leicester (Cen.) 8 20 a.m. (Table 1) — Dep. Sowerby Bridge 9 45 a.m. (Table 33) — Dep. Silkstone 10 2 a.m. (Table 34) — Dep. Worcester (S.H.) 7 15 a.m. (Table 34) — Dep. Sheffield (Vic.) 10 55 a.m. (Table 34) — Dep. Liverpool (Ex.) 9 3 a.m. (Table 33) — Dep. Manchester (L.Rd) 9 45 a.m. (Table 34) — Dep. Basford & Bulwell 9 42 a.m. (Table 15) — Dep. Newcastle 10 25 a.m. (Tables 65 and 50) — Dep. Selby 2 30 p.m. (Table 25) — Dep. York 2 55 p.m. (Tables 18 and 25) — Dep. King's Cross 11 0 a.m. (Table 15)

A timetable from 1949

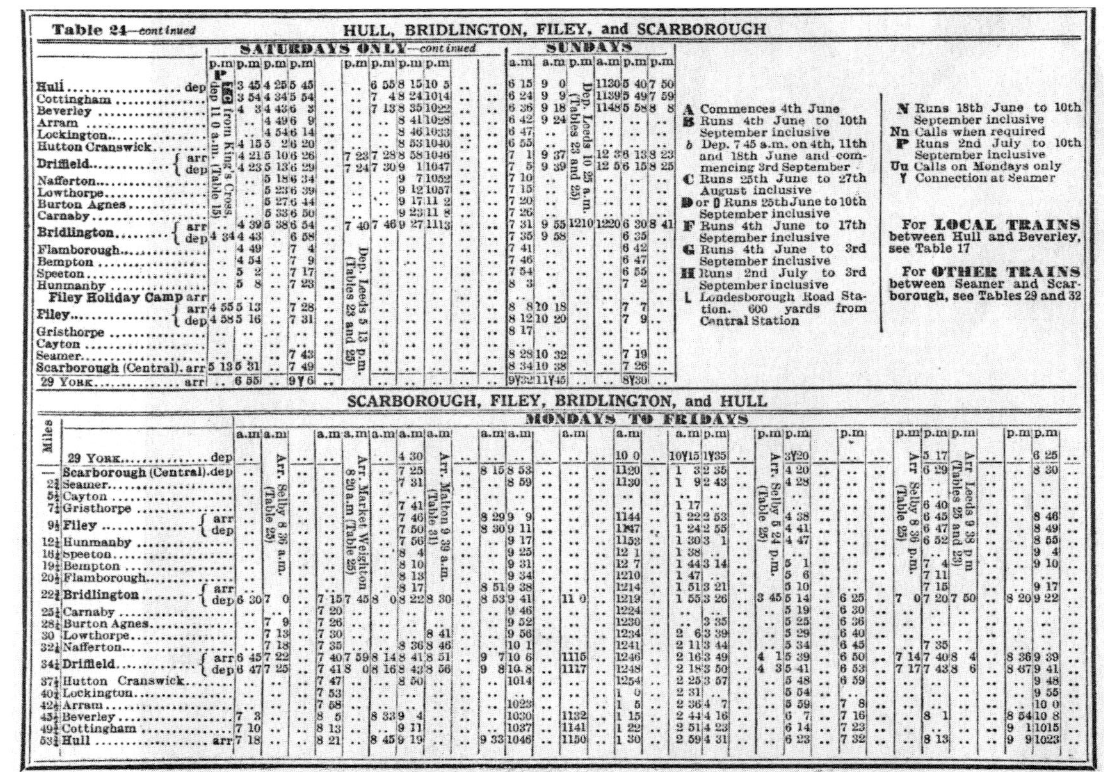

Table 24—*continued*

HULL, BRIDLINGTON, FILEY, and SCARBOROUGH

SATURDAYS ONLY—*continued*

	P p.m	p.m	p.m	p.m		p.m	p.m	p.m	p.m		
Hull ... dep	TC from King's Cross, dep 11 0 a.m. (Table 15)	3 45	4 25	5 45	..	..	6 55	8 15	10 5	..	..
Cottingham		3 54	4 34	5 54	..	..	7 4	8 24	1014	..	..
Beverley		4 3	4 43	6 3	..	..	7 13	8 35	1022	..	..
Arram		..	4 49	6 9	..	..	..	8 41	1028	..	..
Lockington		..	4 54	6 14	..	..	..	8 46	1033	..	..
Hutton Cranswick		4 15	5 2	6 20	..	..	..	8 53	1040	..	..
Driffield ... arr		4 21	5 10	6 26	..	7 23	7 28	8 58	1046	..	..
Driffield ... dep		4 23	5 13	6 29	..	7 24	7 30	9 1	1047	..	..
Nafferton		..	5 18	6 34	..	..	..	9 7	1052	..	..
Lowthorpe		..	5 23	6 39	..	..	..	9 12	1057	..	..
Burton Agnes		..	5 27	6 44	..	..	..	9 17	11 2	..	..
Carnaby		..	5 33	6 50	..	..	..	9 23	11 8	..	..
Bridlington ... arr	..	4 39	5 38	6 54	..	7 40	7 46	9 27	1113	..	..
Bridlington ... dep	4 34	4 43	..	6 58	..	Dep. Leeds 5 13 p.m. (Tables 23 and 25)	..	..	..	..	..
Flamborough	..	4 49	..	7 4	..		..	..	..	..	..
Bempton	..	4 54	..	7 9	..		..	..	..	..	..
Speeton	..	5 2	..	7 17	..		..	..	..	..	..
Hunmanby	..	5 8	..	7 23	..		..	..	..	..	..
Filey Holiday Camp arr	..	..	..	..	..		..	..	..	..	..
Filey ... arr	4 55	5 13	..	7 28	..		..	..	..	..	..
Filey ... dep	4 58	5 16	..	7 31	..		..	..	..	..	..
Gristhorpe	..	..	..	..	..		..	..	..	..	..
Cayton	..	..	..	..	..		..	..	..	..	..
Seamer	..	..	..	7 43	..		..	..	..	..	..
Scarborough (Central). arr	5 13	5 31	..	7 49	..		..	..	..	..	..
29 York ... arr	..	6 55	..	9Y6	..		..	..	..	..	..

SUNDAYS

	a.m	a.m	p.m	a.m	p.m	p.m
Hull ... dep	6 15	9 0	Dep. Leeds 10 25 a.m. (Tables 23 and 25)	1130	5 40	7 50
Cottingham	6 24	9 9		1139	5 49	7 59
Beverley	6 36	9 18		1148	5 58	8 8
Arram	6 42	9 24		..	..	..
Lockington	6 47	..		..	..	..
Hutton Cranswick	6 55	..		..	..	..
Driffield ... arr	7 1	9 37		12 3	6 13	8 23
Driffield ... dep	7 5	9 39		12 5	6 15	8 25
Nafferton	7 10	..		..	..	..
Lowthorpe	7 15	..		..	..	..
Burton Agnes	7 20	..		..	..	..
Carnaby	7 26	..		..	..	..
Bridlington ... arr	7 31	9 55	1210	1220	6 30	8 41
Bridlington ... dep	7 35	9 58	..	..	6 35	..
Flamborough	7 41	..	..	..	6 42	..
Bempton	7 46	..	..	..	6 47	..
Speeton	7 54	..	..	..	6 55	..
Hunmanby	8 3	..	..	..	7 2	..
Filey Holiday Camp arr	..	..	..	..	..	..
Filey ... arr	8 8	10 18	..	..	7 7	..
Filey ... dep	8 12	10 20	..	..	7 9	..
Gristhorpe	8 17	..	..	..	..	..
Cayton	..	..	..	..	..	..
Seamer	8 28	10 32	..	..	7 19	..
Scarborough (Central). arr	8 34	10 38	..	..	7 26	..
29 York ... arr	9Y32	11Y45	..	..	8Y30	..

A Commences 4th June
B Runs 4th June to 10th September inclusive
b Dep. 7 45 a.m. on 4th, 11th and 18th June and commencing 3rd September
C Runs 25th June to 27th August inclusive
D or **D** Runs 25th June to 10th September inclusive
F Runs 4th June to 17th September inclusive
G Runs 4th June to 3rd September inclusive
H Runs 2nd July to 3rd September inclusive
L Londesborough Road Station. 600 yards from Central Station

N Runs 18th June to 10th September inclusive
Nn Calls when required
P Runs 2nd July to 10th September inclusive
Uu Calls on Mondays only
Y Connection at Seamer

For **LOCAL TRAINS** between Hull and Beverley, see Table 17

For **OTHER TRAINS** between Seamer and Scarborough, see Tables 29 and 32

SCARBOROUGH, FILEY, BRIDLINGTON, and HULL

MONDAYS TO FRIDAYS

Miles		a.m	a.m		a.m	a.m	a.m	a.m	a.m		a.m
	29 York ... dep	..	Arr. Selby 8 36 a.m. (Table 25)	..	..	Arr. Market Weighton 8 20 a.m (Table 25)	..	4 30	Arr. Malton 9 39 a.m. (Table 31)	..	..
—	**Scarborough** (Central).dep	..		..	..		..	7 25		..	8 15
2¾	Seamer	..		..	..		..	7 31		..	..
5½	Cayton	..		..	..		..	..		..	..
7½	Gristhorpe	..		..	..		..	7 41		..	..
9½	**Filey** ... arr	..		..	..		..	7 46		..	8 29
	Filey ... dep	..		..	..		..	7 50		..	8 30
12½	Hunmanby	..		..	..		..	7 56		..	..
16½	Speeton	..		..	..		..	8 4		..	..
19½	Bempton	..		..	..		..	8 10		..	..
20½	Flamborough	..		..	..		..	8 13		..	..
22¾	**Bridlington** ... arr	..		..	..		..	8 17		..	8 51
	Bridlington ... dep	6 30	7 0	..	7 15	7 45	8 0	8 22	8 30	..	8 53
25½	Carnaby	..	..	..	7 20	..	..	..	..	..	..
28½	Burton Agnes	..	7 9	..	7 26	..	..	..	..	..	..
30	Lowthorpe	..	7 13	..	7 30	..	..	..	8 41	..	..
32½	Nafferton	..	7 18	..	7 35	..	..	8 36	8 46	..	..
34½	**Driffield** ... arr	6 45	7 22	..	7 40	7 59	8 14	8 41	8 51	..	9 7
	Driffield ... dep	6 47	7 25	..	7 41	8 0	8 16	8 43	8 56	..	9 8
37½	Hutton Cranswick	..	..	..	7 47	..	..	8 50	..	..	..
40½	Lockington	..	..	..	7 53	..	..	..	..	..	..
42½	Arram	..	..	..	7 58	..	..	..	..	..	..
45½	Beverley	7 3	..	..	8 5	..	8 33	9 4	..	..	..
49½	Cottingham	7 10	..	..	8 13	..	..	9 11	..	..	..
53½	**Hull** ... arr	7 18	..	..	8 21	..	8 45	9 19	..	..	9 33

Miles		a.m		a.m		a.m		a.m	p.m		p.m
	29 York ... dep	..	..	..	..	10 0	..	10Y15	1Y35	..	Arr. Selby 5 24 p.m. (Table 25)
—	**Scarborough** (Central).dep	8 53	..	..	..	1120	..	1 3	2 35	..	
2¾	Seamer	8 59	..	..	..	1130	..	1 9	2 43	..	
5½	Cayton	..	..	..	..	..	..	..	..	..	
7½	Gristhorpe	..	..	..	..	..	..	1 17	..	..	
9½	**Filey** ... arr	9 9	..	..	..	1144	..	1 22	2 53	..	
	Filey ... dep	9 11	..	..	..	1147	..	1 24	2 55	..	
12½	Hunmanby	9 17	..	..	..	1153	..	1 30	3 1	..	
16½	Speeton	9 25	..	..	..	12 1	..	1 38	..	..	
19½	Bempton	9 31	..	..	..	12 7	..	1 44	3 14	..	
20½	Flamborough	9 34	..	..	..	1210	..	1 47	..	..	
22¾	**Bridlington** ... arr	9 38	..	..	..	1214	..	1 51	3 21	..	
	Bridlington ... dep	9 41	..	11 0	..	1219	..	1 55	3 26	..	3 45
25½	Carnaby	9 46	..	..	..	1224	..	..	..	..	..
28½	Burton Agnes	9 52	..	..	..	1230	..	..	3 35	..	..
30	Lowthorpe	9 56	..	..	..	1234	..	2 6	3 39	..	..
32½	Nafferton	10 1	..	..	..	1241	..	2 11	3 44	..	..
34½	**Driffield** ... arr	10 6	..	1115	..	1246	..	2 16	3 49	..	4 1
	Driffield ... dep	10 8	..	1117	..	1248	..	2 18	3 50	..	4 3
37½	Hutton Cranswick	1014	..	..	..	1254	..	2 25	3 57	..	..
40½	Lockington	..	..	..	..	1 0	..	2 31	..	..	..
42½	Arram	1023	..	..	..	1 5	..	2 36	4 7	..	..
45½	Beverley	1030	..	1132	..	1 15	..	2 44	4 16	..	..
49½	Cottingham	1037	..	1141	..	1 22	..	2 51	4 23	..	..
53½	**Hull** ... arr	1046	..	1150	..	1 30	..	2 59	4 31	..	..

Miles		p.m		p.m		p.m	p.m	p.m		p.m	p.m	
	29 York ... dep	3Y20	..	..	..	Arr Selby 8 36 p.m. (Table 25)	5 17	Arr Leeds 9 38 p m (Tables 25 and 23)	..	..	6 25	..
—	**Scarborough** (Central).dep	4 20	..	..	..		6 29		..	..	8 30	..
2¾	Seamer	4 28	..	..	..		..		..	..	..	..
5½	Cayton	..	..	..	..		..		..	..	..	..
7½	Gristhorpe	..	..	..	..		6 40		..	..	..	..
9½	**Filey** ... arr	4 38	..	..	..		6 45		..	..	8 46	..
	Filey ... dep	4 41	..	..	..		6 47		..	..	8 49	..
12½	Hunmanby	4 47	..	..	..		6 52		..	..	8 55	..
16½	Speeton	..	..	..	..		..		..	..	9 4	..
19½	Bempton	5 1	..	..	..		7 4		..	..	9 10	..
20½	Flamborough	5 6	..	..	..		7 11		..	..	..	..
22¾	**Bridlington** ... arr	5 10	..	..	..		7 15		..	..	9 17	..
	Bridlington ... dep	5 14	..	6 25	..	7 0	7 20	7 50	..	8 20	9 22	..
25½	Carnaby	5 19	..	6 30	..	..	..	..	..	..	..	..
28½	Burton Agnes	5 25	..	6 36	..	..	..	..	..	..	..	..
30	Lowthorpe	5 29	..	6 40	..	..	..	..	..	..	..	..
32½	Nafferton	5 34	..	6 45	..	..	7 35	..	..	..	..	..
34½	**Driffield** ... arr	5 39	..	6 50	..	7 14	7 40	8 4	..	8 36	9 39	..
	Driffield ... dep	5 41	..	6 53	..	7 17	7 43	8 6	..	8 37	9 41	..
37½	Hutton Cranswick	5 48	..	6 59	..	..	..	..	..	..	9 48	..
40½	Lockington	5 54	..	..	..	..	..	..	..	..	9 55	..
42½	Arram	5 59	..	7 8	..	..	..	..	..	..	10 0	..
45½	Beverley	6 7	..	7 16	..	..	8 1	..	..	8 54	10 8	..
49½	Cottingham	6 14	..	7 23	..	..	..	..	..	9 1	1015	..
53½	**Hull** ... arr	6 23	..	7 32	..	..	8 13	..	..	9 9	1023	..

Continuation of a 1942 timetable

services between Beverley and Hull, no doubt increased due to war workers. Of these, 4-5 were worked by the Sentinel steam railcars which were no longer green and cream but either had this obliterated by layers of oily neglect or, like "Hero", one of the number, appeared in a coach brown livery. Failures would lead to an old steam engine being pressed into service with an ancient coach attached. Yes, there were services on Sunday, with two railcar turns. Fast turns of speed were not aimed at, though the 8am. ex Bridlington features, as does the 5pm. from Hull, fast to Bridlington but continuing to Scarborough.

1949

This was one of the rosiest years for the line, perhaps for railways generally. The timetable will speak for itself, particularly the Saturdays Only section for the holiday traffic, with eight returns from Filey Camp, beginning at 8.35am. to Newcastle, York, Birmingham, York, Sheffield, King's Cross, Leeds, and Manchester Exch. There were returns to Manchester London Rd. and Silkstone from Scarborough, followed by the important 11.55pm. to Leicester Cen. which was almost aways double-headed, running ahead of a Liverpool Exch. and a Derby. The solitary Bridlington weekly departure in the midst of this flurry was the 1.15pm. which reached Rotherham & Masborough at 3.47pm., probably hauled by a 4F 0-6-0 goods engine. The arrivals came from different places in some cases, such as Worcester Shrub Hill, Sowerby Bridge and Chesterfield, not forgetting Basford & Bulwell. Careful scrutiny will shows services to and from the Selby-Market Weighton line, and one run between Bridlington and Malton via the Burdale branch line.

1951

One hundred years of travel on the line is completed by a look at the December 1951 timetable, with 8-9 trains each way the whole length of the line on weekdays and two on Sundays, the fastest being the 8.15am. from Scarborough, reaching Hull at 9.38am., and the 5.10pm. ex Hull reaching

Scarborough at 6.29pm. There were 6-7 trains which ran between Bridlington and Hull only, including the famous 8am. Up and 5pm. Down. The Hull-Beverley service could still total 37 each way, all steam hauled by G5s or C12s at this time, while the trains to and from Market Weighton augmented the flow north of Driffield.

It was not many years now before the first diesel units arrived on the scene, finding the 40 min. run between Hull and Bridlington hard to equal.

2000

With the second generation of dmus, has come a regular interval service, with 18 trains from Bridlington at 18 min. and 48 min. past the hour and 16 to Bridlington at 23 min. and 53 min. past, though the sequence is broken by the slotting in of the Scarborough trains. There are 9-10 of these, and some attempt has been made to synchronise them with the Bridlington trains. One might say that all trains stop everywhere, except for Arram which has only six calls from Hull and four the other way. Hutton Cranswick also misses a few calls. The present run to Bridlington, with all stops is 48min., while the Scarborough run is 1hr. 23mins.

There are still lingering remnants of local services to Beverley, though the total of all trains calling there is still 37 trains each way. There is a 6.45am. from Beverley to Hull, and a 7.01 which runs through to Manchester Airport. Later, at 9.28 a service leaves Beverley for Sheffield, joining two others during the day which extend to Sheffield either from Scarborough or Bridlington. The habit is catching, as the 6.58am. starts at Filey, then runs to Scarborough and reverses to carry on to Manchester Airport. During the day three services run on either to Bridlington or Beverley from Sheffield. One oddment runs through to Beverley from Middlesbrough. The Sunday services are basically four trains to and from Bridlington, with a full service of six trains to and from Bridlington originating at Sheffield and six to Scarborough in the season.

Table 24—*continued*

SCARBOROUGH, FILEY, BRIDLINGTON, and HULL

SATURDAYS ONLY

	a.m	a.m	a.m	a.m	a.m	a.m	a.m	a.m	a.m Q	a.m U	a.m	a.m J	a.m	a.m J	a.m	a.m
29 York .... dep	..		..		..	4 30		..	..	..	..	..	..	..	..	..
Scarborough (Central) .dep	..	Arr. Selby 8 36 a.m. (Table 25)	..	Arr. Market Weighton 8 20 a.m (Table 25)	..	7 25	Arr Malton 9 39 a.m. (Table 31)	8 15	..	..	8 53	..	..	..	..	..
Seamer	..		..		..	7 31		..	..	..	8 59	..	..	..	..	..
Cayton	..		..		..	..		..	..	..	..	..	..	..	..	..
Gristhorpe	..		..		..	7 41		..	..	..	..	..	..	..	..	..
Filey .... arr	..		..		..	7 46		8 29	..	..	9 9	..	..	..	..	..
Filey .... dep	..		..		..	7 50		8 30	..	..	9 11	..	..	..	..	..
Filey Holiday Camp	..		..		..	..		..	8 35	9 0	..	9 30	9 45	1010	..	..
Hunmanby	..		..		..	7 56		..	..	..	9 17	..	..	..	..	..
Speeton	..		..		..	8 4		..	..	..	9 25	..	..	..	..	..
Bempton	..		..		..	8 10		..	..	..	9 31	..	..	..	..	..
Flamborough	..		..		..	8 13		..	..	..	9 34	..	..	..	..	..
Bridlington .... arr	..		..		..	8 17		8 51	8 57	9 27	9 38	9 53	10 7	1033	..	..
Bridlington .... dep	6 30	7 0	7 15	7 45	8 0	8 22	8 30	8 53	9 2	9 32	9 41	9 58	1012	1038	1050	11 0
Carnaby	..	..	7 20	..	..	..	..	..	Arr Newcastle 1 15 p m (Tables 50 and 65)	Arr. York 10 50 a.m (Tables 25 and 18)	9 46	Arr. Birmingham 2 58 p.m (Table 34)	Arr. York 11 19 a.m. (Tables 25 and 18)	Arr. Sheffield (Vic.) 1 11 p.m. (Table 34)	Arr. Leeds 12 31 p.m (Tables 25 and 23)	..
Burton Agnes	..	7 9	7 26	..	..	..	..	..			9 52					..
Lowthorpe	..	7 13	7 30	..	..	..	8 41	..			9 56					..
Nafferton	..	7 18	7 35	..	..	8 36	8 46	..			10 1					..
Driffield .... arr	6 45	7 22	7 40	7 59	8 14	8 41	8 51	9 7			10 6					1115
Driffield .... dep	6 47	7 25	7 41	8 0	8 16	8 43	8 56	9 8			10 8					1117
Hutton Cranswick	..	..	7 47	..	..	8 50	..	..			1014					..
Lockington	..	..	7 53	..	..	..	..	..			..					..
Arram	..	..	7 58	..	..	..	..	..			1023					..
Beverley	7 3	..	8 5	..	8 33	9 4	..	..			1030					1132
Cottingham	7 10	..	8 13	..	..	9 11	..	..			1037					1141
Hull .... arr	7 18	..	8 21	..	8 45	9 19	..	9 33			1046					1150

	a.m. N	a.m K	a.m. F	a.m. N	a.m	a.m	a.m	a.m. F	p.m Q	p.m A	p.m Q	a.m N	p.m	p.m A	p.m P
29 York .... dep	..	..	..	..	10 0	..	10Y15	..	..	..	..	1135	..	..	..
Scarborough (Central) .dep	10L15	..	..	10L50	1110	..	1120	11L55	1215	..	..	1255	1 3	..	..
Seamer	..	..	..	..	..	..	1130	..	..	..	..	..	1 9	..	..
Cayton	..	..	..	..	..	..	1136	..	..	Arr. Rotherham and Masboro' 3 47 p.m. (Table 15)	..	..	..	..	..
Gristhorpe	..	..	..	..	..	..	1141	..	..		..	..	1 17	..	..
Filey .... arr	10 30	..	..	11 5	1126	..	1146	12 10	1231		..	1 10	1 22	..	..
Filey .... dep	10 33	..	..	11 8	1129	..	1149	12 13	1236		..	1 15	1 24	..	..
Filey Holiday Camp	..	1050	..	..	..	1137	..	..	..		1255	..	..	..	..
Hunmanby	..	..	..	..	..	..	1155	..	..		..	..	1 30	..	..
Speeton	..	..	..	..	..	..	12 3	..	..		..	..	1 38	..	..
Bempton	..	..	..	..	..	..	12 9	..	..		..	..	1 44	..	..
Flamborough	..	..	..	..	..	..	1212	..	..		..	..	1 47	..	..
Bridlington .... arr	10 57	1113	..	11 30	1153	12 0	1216	12 35	1 0		1 19	1 37	1 51	..	..
Bridlington .... dep	11 7	1118	11 27	11 35	1156	12 3	1221	12 40	1 5	1 15	1 25	1 42	1 55	2 12	2 20
Carnaby	Arr. Manchester (L.R.) 3 5 p.m. (Table 34)	Arr. King's Cross 4 30 p.m. (Table 15)	Arr. Sheffield (Vic.) 2 13 p.m. (Table 15)	Arr. Silkstone 2 40 p.m. (Table 34)	..	Arr. Leeds 1 48 p.m. (Table 25 and 23)	1226	Arr. Leicester (Cen.) 5 25 p.m. (Table 34)	Arr. Liverpool (Ex.) 5 40 p.m. (Table 33)	..	Arr. Manchester (Ex.) 4 43 p.m. (Table 23)	Arr. Derby 5 32 p.m. (Table 34)	..	Arr. Sheffield (Vic.) 4 57 p.m. (Table 34)	Arr. Leeds 4 6 p.m (Tables 25 and 23)
Burton Agnes					..		1232			..			..		
Lowthorpe					..		1236			..			2 6		
Nafferton					..		1243			..			2 11		
Driffield .... arr					1212		1248			..			2 16		
Driffield .... dep					1214		1250			..			2 18		
Hutton Cranswick					..		1256			..			2 25		
Lockington					..		1 2			..			2 31		
Arram					..		1 7			..			2 36		
Beverley					1232		1 17			..			2 44		
Cottingham					..		1 24			..			2 51		
Hull .... arr					1245		1 32			..			2 59		

SATURDAYS ONLY—*continued*

	p.m F	p.m D	p.m H	p.m	p.m C	p.m C	p.m	p.m D	p.m	p.m	p.m	p.m	p.m	p.m	p.m	p.m	
29 York .... dep	..	..	..	1Y37	..	..		..	3Y20	..	4P45		5 17	..	6 25	..	..
Scarborough (Central) .dep	..	..	2L18	2 35	2 45	2L57	Arr. Selby 5 32 p.m. (Table 25)	3 55	4 20	..	6 0	Arr. Leeds 9 32 p.m. (Tables 25 and 23)	6 29	..	8 30	..	..
Seamer	..	..	..	2 43	..	..		..	4 28	..	..		..	..	..	..	..
Cayton	..	..	..	..	..	..		..	..	..	..		..	..	..	..	..
Gristhorpe	..	..	..	..	..	..		..	..	..	..		6 40	..	..	..	..
Filey .... arr	..	..	2 33	2 53	3 2	3 13		4 11	4 38	..	6 16		6 45	..	8 46	..	..
Filey .... dep	..	..	2 36	2 55	3 5	3 17		4 15	4 41	..	6 19		6 47	..	8 49	..	..
Filey Holiday Camp	..	..	..	..	..	..		..	..	..	..		..	..	..	..	..
Hunmanby	..	..	..	3 1	..	..		..	4 47	..	..		6 52	..	8 55	..	..
Speeton	..	..	..	..	..	..		..	..	..	..		..	..	9 4	..	..
Bempton	..	..	..	3 14	..	..		..	5 1	..	..		7 4	..	9 10	..	..
Flamborough	..	..	..	..	..	..		..	5 6	..	..		7 11	..	..	..	..
Bridlington .... arr	..		2 58	3 21	3 30	3 39		4 39	5 10	..	6 44		7 15	..	9 17	..	..
Bridlington .... dep	2 30	2 50	3 3	3 26	3 35	3 44	4 0	4 45	5 14	6 25	6 50	7 0	7 20	8 20	9 22	11 5	—
Carnaby	Arr. Bradford (Ex.) 5 35 p.m. (Tables 33,7 and 10)	..	Arr. Chesterfield 6 10 p.m. (Table 34)	..	Arr. Sowerby Bridge 6 35 p.m. (Table 33)	Arr. Nottingham (Vic. 7 58 p.m. (Table 15)	..	..	5 19	6 30	..	..	..	..	..	1110	..
Burton Agnes		..		3 35			..	..	5 25	6 36	..	..	..	..	..	1116	..
Lowthorpe		..		3 39			..	..	5 29	6 40	..	..	..	..	..	1120	..
Nafferton		..		3 44			..	..	5 34	6 45	..	..	7 35	..	..	1125	..
Driffield .... arr		3 7		3 49			4 16	5 1	5 39	6 50	7 7	7 14	7 40	8 36	9 39	1130	..
Driffield .... dep		3 10		3 50			4 18	5 4	5 41	6 53	7 10	7 17	7 43	8 37	9 41	1133	..
Hutton Cranswick		..		3 57			..	..	5 48	6 59	..	..	..	..	9 48	1140	..
Lockington		..		..			..	..	5 54	..	..	..	..	..	9 55	..	..
Arram		..		4 7			..	..	5 59	7 8	..	..	..	..	10 0	1149	—
Beverley		3 30		4 16			..	5 24	6 7	7 16	7 30	..	8 1	8 54	10 8	1157	..
Cottingham		..		4 23			..	..	6 14	7 23	..	..	..	9 1	1015	12 6	..
Hull .... arr		3 44		4 31			..	5 39	6 23	7 32	7 44	..	8 13	9 9	1023	1215	..

SUNDAYS

	a.m	a.m	p.m	p.m	p.m	p.m
29 York .... dep	..	9Y5	..	5Y0	..	..
Scarborough (Central) .dep	..	1025	..	6 0	..	8 45
Seamer	..	1032	..	6 7	..	..
Cayton	..	..	..	..	..	..
Gristhorpe	..	1040	..	6 15	..	..
Filey .... arr	..	1045	..	6 20	..	8 59
Filey .... dep	..	1047	..	6 22	..	9 1
Filey Holiday Camp	..	..	..	..	..	..
Hunmanby	..	1053	..	6 29	..	..
Speeton	..	11 1	..	6 38	..	..
Bempton	..	11 7	..	6 44	..	..
Flamborough	..	1110	..	6 49	..	..
Bridlington .... arr	..	1115	..	6 53	..	9 21
Bridlington .... dep	8 10	1120	1 35	7 2	8 35	9 24
Carnaby	..	1125	..	7 7	Arr. Leeds 10 23 p.m. (Tables 25 and 23)	..
Burton Agnes	..	1131	..	7 13		..
Lowthorpe	..	1135	..	7 17		..
Nafferton	..	1140	..	7 22		..
Driffield .... arr	8 25	1145	1 50	7 27		9 40
Driffield .... dep	8 27	1147	1 52	7 30		9 42
Hutton Cranswick	..	1154	..	7 37		..
Lockington	..	12 2	..	7 44		..
Arram	..	1210	..	7 49		..
Beverley	8 44	1218	2 9	7 58		9 59
Cottingham	8 51	1226	2 16	8 5		..
Hull .... arr	9 0	1235	2 25	8 14		1012

A Commences 4th June
C Runs 25th June to 27th August inclusive
D Runs 25th June to 10th September inclusive
F Runs 4th June to 17th September inclusive
H Runs 2nd July to 3rd September inclusive
J Runs 11th June to 17th September inclusive
K Commences 9th July
L Londesborough Road Station. 600 yards from Central Station
N Runs 18th June to 10th September inclusive
P or P Runs 2nd July to 10th September inclusive
Q Runs 11th June to 10th September inclusive
U Runs only on 28th May, 4th June and, 24th September

For **LOCAL TRAINS** between Beverley and Hull, see Table 17

For **OTHER TRAINS** between Scarborough and Seamer, see Tables 29 and 32

Up services in1949 timetable

Table 24 — **HULL, BRIDLINGTON, FILEY, and SCARBOROUGH**

Week Days

Miles	Station		a.m	a.m	a.m	a.m	a.m (Dep. Market Weighton 8 55 a.m. (Table 25))	a.m (Dep. Selby 9 20 a.m. (Table 25))	a.m
—	**Hull**	dep	5 30	5 55	7 38	8 35			10 35
4	Cottingham		..	..	7 46	8 44			10 44
8¼	Beverley		..	..	7 55	8 54			10 53
11¼	Arram		5 49	..	8 1	..			10 59
13	Lockington		..	6 15	8 6	..			..
16¼	Hutton Cranswick		..	6 21	8 12	..			11 9
19¼	**Driffield**	arr	6 1	6 27	8 18	9 9	9 17	1032	11 15
		dep	6 7	6 33	8 20	9 11	9 19	1034	11 16
21¼	Nafferton		..	6 38	8 26			1040	11 21
23	Lowthorpe		..	6 43	8 31				11 27
25¼	Burton Agnes		6 17	..	8 35			1046	..
28½	Carnaby		..	6 51	8 41				11 35
31	**Bridlington**	arr	6 25	6 56	8 46	9 27	9 35	1054	11 40
		dep	6 35	..	8 51	9 30			11 43
33½	Flamborough		..	..	8 58				11 49
34½	Bempton		6 46	..	9 4				11 54
37¼	Speeton		..	..	9 13				..
41½	Hunmanby		6 59	..	9 21				12 7
44½	**Filey**	arr	7 4	..	9 26	9 52			12 13
		dep	7 11	..	9 31	9 55			12 14
46¼	Gristhorpe		..	..	9 36				..
48½	Cayton			..	9S41				
51	Seamer		7 22	..		10 7			12 27
53¾	**Scarborough** (Central)	arr	7 31		9B48	10 15			12 33
95½	29 York	arr	9 4		11[illegible]	11Y[illegible]			1Y40

Station		p.m	p.m S	p.m	p.m	p.m	p.m E	p.m E	p.m E (Dep. Market Weighton 5 55 p.m. (Table 25))	p.m	p.m E (Dep. Leeds 5 7 p.m. (Tables 23 and 25))
Hull	dep	12 25	12 50	1 20	3 42	4 25	5 10	5 30		5 45	
Cottingham		12 34	..	1 29	3 50	4 34	..	..		5 54	
Beverley		12 43	1 4	1 39	3 59	4 43	5 23	5 43		6 3	
Arram		..	..	1 46	..	4 49	..	..		6 9	
Lockington		..	..	1 51	..	4 54	..	..		6 14	
Hutton Cranswick				1 58	..	5 2				6 20	
Driffield	arr	12 59	1 20	2 4	4 13	5 10	5 36	5 56	6 18	6 26	6 35
	dep	1 1	1 21	2 7	4 15	5 13	5 37	5 59	6 19	6 29	6 37
Nafferton			..	2 13	..	5 18	..	..		6 34	..
Lowthorpe				2 18	..	5 23				6 39	..
Burton Agnes			..	2 23	..	5 27	..	..		6 44	..
Carnaby				2 29	..	5 33				6 50	
Bridlington	arr	1 16	1 38	2 34	4 31	5 38	5 51	6 15	6 35	6 54	6 58
	dep		1 43	2 40	4 34	..	5 53	..		7 1	
Flamborough			1 51	..	4 40	..	..	..		7 7	
Bempton			1 56	..	4 45	..	..	..		7 12	
Speeton			..	..	4 53	..	..	..		7 20	
Hunmanby			..	..	4 59	..	..	..		7 26	
Filey	arr		2 13	3 2	5 4	..	6 15	..		7 31	
	dep		2 17	3 7	5 7	..	6 16	..		7 34	
Gristhorpe			..	Nn	..	..	..	..		..	
Cayton			..	..	..	..	..	..		..	
Seamer				3 18	..	..	..	..		7 46	
Scarborough (Central)	arr		2 32	3 27	5 22		6 30			7 52	
29 York	arr			4Y30						9Y 3	

Station		p.m	p.m (Dep. Selby 6 20 p.m. (Table 25))	p.m	p.m	Sundays a.m	Sundays a.m	Sundays p.m	Sundays p.m
Hull	dep	6 47		8 10	9 45	6 15	1130	5 40	7 50
Cottingham		6 56		8 19	9 54	6 23	1139	5 49	7 59
Beverley		7 5		8‡30	10 3	6‡35	1148	5 58	8 8
Arram		..		8 36	10 8	6 41	..	..	..
Lockington		..		8 41	1013	6 46	..	..	..
Hutton Cranswick		..		8 48	1020	6 54	..	..	..
Driffield	arr	7 20	7 34	8 53	1024	7 0	12 3	6 13	8 23
	dep	7 22	7 35	8 56	1027	7 4	12 5	6 15	8 25
Nafferton		..		9 2	1033	7 9	..	..	..
Lowthorpe		..		9 7	1037	7 14	..	..	..
Burton Agnes		..		9 12	1043	7 19	..	..	..
Carnaby		..		9 18	1049	7 25	..	..	..
Bridlington	arr	7 38	7 51	9 22	1053	7 30	1220	6 30	8 41
	dep	..		..	..	7K34	..	6 35	..
Flamborough		..		..	..	7K40	..	6 42	..
Bempton		..		..	..	7K45	..	6 47	..
Speeton		..		..	..	7K53	..	6 55	..
Hunmanby		..		..	..	8K2	..	7 2	..
Filey	arr	..		..	..	8K7	..	7 7	..
	dep	..		..	..	8K11	..	7 9	..
Gristhorpe		..		..	..	8K16	..	..	..
Cayton		..		..	..	..	..	..	..
Seamer		..		..	..	8K27	..	7 21	..
Scarborough (Central)	arr	..		..	..	8K33	..	7 27	..
29 York	arr					11K42		8Y30	

Week Days

Miles	Station		a.m	a.m (Arr. Selby 8 36 a.m. (Table 25))	a.m	a.m (Arr. Market Weighton 8 20 a.m. (Table 25))	a.m	a.m	a.m	a.m
	29 York	dep						4 30		
—	**Scarborough** (Central)	dep	..		..		..	7 25	8 15	8 29
2¾	Seamer		..		..		..	7 31	..	8 34
5¼	Cayton		..		..		..	..	..	..
7¼	Gristhorpe		..		..		..	7 41	..	..
9¼	**Filey**	arr	..		..		..	7 46	8 29	8 44
		dep	..		..		..	7 49	8 30	8 45
12¼	Hunmanby		..		..		..	7 55	..	8 51
16¼	Speeton		..		..		..	8 3	..	..
19¼	Bempton		..		..		..	8 9	..	9 3
20½	Flamborough		..		..		..	8 12	..	9 6
22½	**Bridlington**	arr	..				..	8 16	8 51	9 10
		dep	6 30	7 0	7 15	7 45	8 0	8 20	8 53	9 12
25¼	Carnaby		..	..	7 20	..	..	..	..	9 17
28¼	Burton Agnes		..	7 9	7 26	..	..	..	..	9 23
30	Lowthorpe		..	7 13	7 30	..	..	8 31	..	9 27
32¼	Nafferton		..	7 18	7 35	..	..	8 36	..	9 32
34¼	**Driffield**	arr	6 45	7 22	7 40	7 59	8 14	8 41	9 7	9 37
		dep	6 47	7 25	7 41	8 0	8 15	8 43	9 8	9 39
37¼	Hutton Cranswick		..	..	7 47	..	..	8 50	..	9 45
40¾	Lockington		..	..	7 53	..	..	..	..	..
42¼	Arram		..	..	7 58	..	..	..	..	9 54
45¼	Beverley		7 3	..	8 5	..	8 30	9 4	..	10 1
49¾	Cottingham		7 10	..	8 13	..	8 37	9 11	..	10 8
53¾	**Hull**	arr	7 18	..	8 21		8 45	9 19	9 33	1016

Station		a.m	a.m	p.m	p.m	p.m E (Arr. Market Weighton 5 26 p.m. (Table 25))	p.m	p.m
29 York	dep		10 15		1 30		2 55	..
Scarborough (Central)	dep	..	11 30	1 3	2 40		4 30	..
Seamer		..	11 37	1 9	2 48		4 37	..
Cayton		..	Dd	..	..		..	..
Gristhorpe		..	Dd	1 17	..		..	..
Filey	arr	..	11U51	1 22	2 58		4 47	..
	dep	..	11U54	1 24	3 0		4 49	..
Hunmanby		..	12U0	1 30	3 6		4 55	..
Speeton		..	..	1 38	..		..	..
Bempton		..	12U13	1 44	3 19		5 9	..
Flamborough		..	12U16	1 47	..		5 14	..
Bridlington	arr	..	12U20	1 51	3 26		5 18	..
	dep	10 52	12U24	1 55	3 31	4 40	5 23	6 25
Carnaby		..	..	2 0	..	4 45	5 28	6 30
Burton Agnes		..	12U33	..	3 40	4 51	5 34	6 36
Lowthorpe		..	12U37	2 8	3 44	4 55	5 38	6 40
Nafferton		..	12U42	2 13	3 49	5 0	5 43	6 45
Driffield	arr	11 7	12U47	2 18	3 54	5 5	5 48	6 50
	dep	11 9	12U49	2 20	3 55	5 6	5 51	6 53
Hutton Cranswick		..	12U55	2 26	4 2	..	5 58	6 59
Lockington		..	1U1	2 32	4 8	..	6 4	..
Arram		..	1U6	2 37	4 13	..	6 10	7 8
Beverley		11 24	1U15	2 45	4 21	..	6 17	7 16
Cottingham		11 31	1U22	2 52	4 28	..	6 24	7 23
Hull	arr	11 39	1U30	3 0	4 36	..	6 32	7 31

Station		p.m (Arr. Selby 8 41 p.m. (Table 25))	p.m	p.m	p.m S	Sundays a.m	Sundays a.m	Sundays p.m	Sundays p.m
29 York	dep		5 8	..	..	..	9K0		5Y0
Scarborough (Central)	dep		6 20	..	..	..	10K25	..	6 0
Seamer			6 26	..	..	..	10K32	..	6 7
Cayton			..	..	..	..		..	..
Gristhorpe			6 34	..	..	..	10K40	..	6 15
Filey	arr		6 39	..	..	..	10K45	..	6 20
	dep		6 41	..	..	..	10K47	..	6 22
Hunmanby			6 46	..	..	..	10K53	..	6 29
Speeton			..	..	..	..	11K1	..	6 38
Bempton			6 58	..	..	..	11K7	..	6 44
Flamborough			7 5	..	..	..	11K10	..	6 49
Bridlington	arr		7 9	..	..	..	11K15	..	6 53
	dep	7 0	7 14	8 20	11 5	8 10	11 20	1 30	7 2
Carnaby		..	..	..	1110	..	11 25	..	7 7
Burton Agnes		..	..	..	1116	..	11 31	..	7 13
Lowthorpe		..	..	..	1120	..	11 35	..	7 17
Nafferton		..	7 27	..	1125	..	11 40	..	7 22
Driffield	arr	7 14	7 32	8 36	1130	8 25	11 45	1 45	7 27
	dep	7 17	7 34	8 37	1133	8 27	11 47	1 47	7 30
Hutton Cranswick		..	..	..	1140	..	11 54	..	7 37
Lockington		..	..	..	..	..	12 2	..	7 44
Arram		..	..	..	1149	..	12 10	..	7 49
Beverley		..	7 50	8 54	1157	8 44	12 18	2 4	7 58
Cottingham		..	..	9 1	12 6	8 51	12 26	2 11	8 5
Hull	arr	..	8 2	9 9	1214	8 59	12 34	2 19	8 13

B Arr. 9 52 a.m. on Saturdays. Dd Calls on Saturdays only. E Except Saturdays. K Commences 6th April, 1952. Nn Calls when required.
S or S Saturdays only. U Runs 2 minutes later on Saturdays. Y Connection at Seamer. ‡ Arr. 4 minutes *earlier*.
For **LOCAL TRAINS** between Hull and Beverley, see Table 17. For **OTHER TRAINS** between Seamer and Scarborough, see Table 29

A timetable from December 1951

AUTOCARS AND SENTINELS

The line was affected at least twice by attempts with passenger railcars. The first was more of an experiment, the second as a much more successful commercial venture. The NER had, in 1903 devised petrol-electric railcar in which a petrol motor drove a dynamo giving an output of 550v. to power two electric motors, for which a fuel tank containing 70 gallons of petrol was required to cover any distance at around 6mpg. Two units of 53ft. 6in. in length and a massive 35 tons 15 cwt. were built, with the power system at one end and the 52 passengers throughout its length on tram type seating. First runs were in the Hartlepools area, after which one of the cars appeared on the Scarborough-Filey section, with six runs during August 1904 at 1/- single (5p) and 1/6d return (8p). The experiment was repeated the following year, this time using both cars. No records exist giving details of the usage of the vehicles, but it is known that they worked during June and July 1908;, after which steam push-and-pull trains took over. The 2.05pm. Scarborough to Filey was the busiest service, and was often steam worked in any case. So it was that a new and often popular innovation fell victim to its own popularity, as were the new dmus. first seen on the the Leeds-Harrogate line in the 50s, often having to be replaced by steam workings due to the volume of passengers wishing to enjoy the new sensation and better all-round views. Eventually the two cars went to Selby for use on the Cawood branch, and a shed was built for them in 1910. Both units were scrapped in 1931, the shed lingering until 1964, when the whole site was cleared.

In 1923 the Sentinel Waggon Works of Shrewsbury built its first steam railcar in collaboration with Cammell, Laird & Co. Nottingham, who built the coachwork. This was intended for the Jersey Railways and was a success. In 1924 a similar railcar was displayed at the Empire Exhibition at Wembley, where it caught the eye of Nigel Gresley, who arranged for the loan of one car for two weeks and, if successful, to purchase two for service use at £3,000 each, a fair price even in those days, though the return would be very good if the cars could be more cheaply worked than a steam train with passengers carried more profitably. Trials were carried out between 17th and 31st August 1924: Gresley and his General Manager Ralph Wedgewood must have been delighted, as some 80 vehicles entered service on the LNER between 1923 and 1932, plus five bought in. Each batch as it appeared was different from the earlier one, as developments were integrated as they arose, always to the good, as the first design seemed all body and no wheels. The length of the cars grew from 57ft. 5in. to 65ft. 8 in., while the weight empty was between 17 tons and 42 tons 12 cwt. After trying out a teak livery on top of the metal sides, vermilion and cream appeared, to be followed, no doubt with all-round relief, by cream and green which was applied to 'Nettle' at Doncaster Works in May 1928, and henceforth to all.

Sentinel' railcar No. 272 'Hero' in wartime brown, makes its mark on the environment at Hull Paragon. *Photo. H C Casserley*

Shunter No. 68145 shunts across the station approach at Bridlington.
Photo. C T Goode

As the result of a public competition, the cars received the names of stage coaches, the first being 'Tally Ho!', each one with a poster framed inside referring to the exploits of the car's namesake. Soon, pleasant flashes of cream could be seen flashing about the countryside in the north east of England, parts of the Midlands and in Scotland, each with its driver and fireman who would double as guard when needed, since he did not need to get too dirty in the hotter part of the car. Here the noise was rather unpleaant, though from the lineside the cars made a quite acceptable chattering noise at speed, similar to the steam road wagons whose mechanisms were, after all, virtually the same.

The first car, 'Valliant' (sic) reached Hull in 1927 and went to work on the Hull-Brough services in 1928, short but intensive. Further cars, 'Tally Ho!', 'High Flyer', 'Eclipse', 'Rockingham' and 'Teazle' went to Botanic Gardens depot in Hull during 1928, followed in the next year by 'Celebrity', 'Cornwallis' and 'Criterion', making a total of eight in all. Most would be occupied, as mentioned, on the Brough service as well as the Beverley runs, less frequent turns to South Howden on the old Hull & Barnsley line and runs out to Withernsea and to Hornsea on Saturdays. At the peak of operations Botanic had nine two cylinder cars and two stronger six cylinder models; 'Tally Ho!', 'High Flyer' and 'Eclipse' served in Hull for the whole of their working lives. There were runs of 31 miles to Bridlington and Thorne North through Goole and, being versatile, the cars were worked hard and often rostered to leave one route for another. The car which worked the fast, first of the day run to Bridlington in 1930 called at Beverley on return to pick up one of the two Clayton four wheel trailers supplied to Hull for use with the cars when needed. This trailer had arrived in Beverley off the previous evening's 6.15pm. run, which obviously merited the extra capacity. Bridlington took over the 6cyl. 'Criterion' in July 1932, which would run various sorties to Selby over the Wolds. There were two round trips on weekdays, leaving Bridlington at 11am. and 3.25pm. On the final leg being completed the car ran empty from Bridlington to Hull and worked a later 10.50pm. back again. After 1933 the empty return became the 8.45pm. stopping train Weds. Only to Hull, getting back to base at 11.46pm. By 1937 the Selby workings had all become four coach steam runs on Mons. and Sats. Only.

Sentinel shunter No. 68155 taking the air at Driffield, north end, on a break from pick-up duties. *Photo. C T Goode*

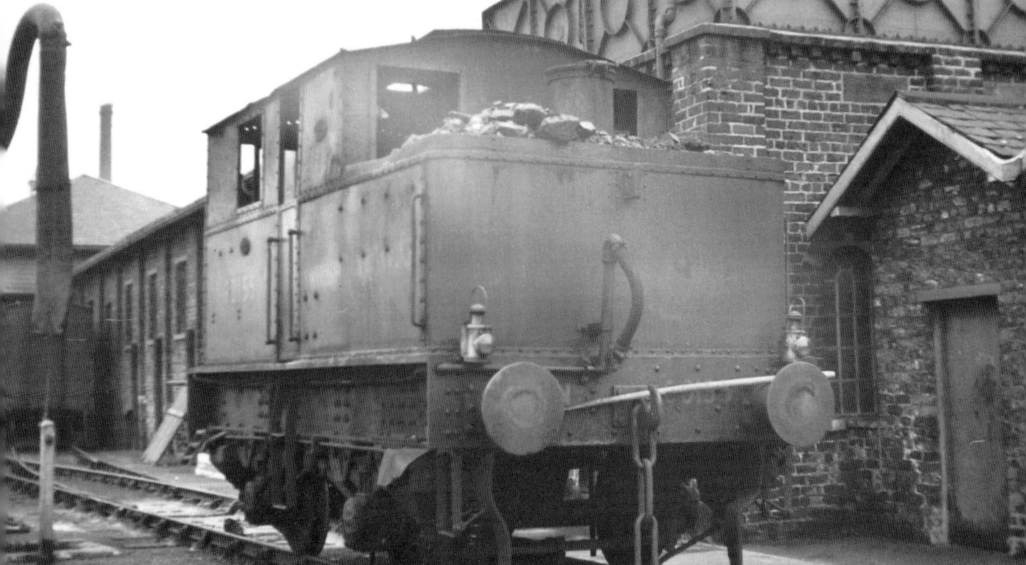

STEAM LOCOMOTIVES

Botanic Gardens was the passenger shed for Hull, being nearer to the station than was Dairycoates which was better placed for servicing the numerous fast freights which ran to and from the dock area. Incidentally, at one time Dairycoates was one of the largest loco. depots in the country both in size and number of engines kept there. It is essential here to avoid the trap of joining the train spotters and resorting to lists of numbers 'on shed' at various times. Sufficient, then, to state that at Grouping, when many small companies became the London & North Eastern Railway, this in April 1923, Botanic shed housed ten D17s, the old racing 4-4-0s which had at one time belted along the stretch between York and Darlington, five D20s which were as good but stronger, 11 D22s and the same number of D23s, many, one suspects, having been offloaded as being of little use elsewhere. To assist with the local workings four C12 4-4-2 tanks were taken in during 1930, followed by five more in the next year.These were Great Northern Doncaster products which worked well on home ground but were disliked by the NER men for their pull-out regulators and temperamental performance. Relief was at hand, though, as in 1932 the shed received six D49s, the new Gresley 4-4-0s which had been tried and tested on heavy main line work and not particularly found wanting. Their numbers were 253, 318, 321, 322, 327 and 335, which were accepted as being reliable, though a rough ride for the crew, a good advert. with the green livery and nameplates. The first batch were named after counties served by the LNER, the second lot after hunts in the region, each plate with a fox depicted over it.

In 1933 Nos. 282 and 292 appeared, followed by
1934 Nos. 205. 214 and 222.
1935 Nos. 230, 238, 283, 318 (again) and 377.
1936 Nos. 220, 256.
1938 Nos. 269, 336.
1939 Nos. 234, 236, 245, 251, 253 (again), 318 (again), 320 and 335 (again).

D49 No. 62769 'The Oakley' waits beneath the roof of Bridlington station, with a service to Scarborough. *Photo. C T Goode*

Repeated numbers seem to indicate that an engine had been transferred away for a time. When it was decided to withdraw the class, the Hull contingent was lined up, along with several B16 4-6-0s at the former H & B shed at Springhead close by. Botanic Gardens shed closed on 14th June 1959, and 25 engines were sent to Dairycoates, the other three, newish B1 4-6-0s Nos. 61068, 61304/5 going to Scarborough. For interest, a list of D49 names to complement the numbers above, appears later.

The final, third version of the loco. shed at Bridlington opened in 1892, of three roads to hold nine engines and complete with a new turntable bought for £385. The site lasted until 1958. Passenger services were worked by the shed to Hull, Scarborough and Leeds, and prior to World War One were worked by older 2-4-0 engines. After 1914 the small NER G 4-4-0s took over, then a batch of Class F (D22) 4-4-0s arrived, working until 1925 when the Class M (D17) 4-4-0s replaced them in turn. An original, the 3 cylinder Smith Compound No. 1619 also came to Bridlington in its green livery, which it retained until withdrawal in 1930. As mentioned, the D17s were fast and used to racing, the 'crack' train here being the 8.05am. Bridlington-Hull which would cover the 31 miles in 37min., unofficially in 34min. if the way into Hull Paragon was clear. Loadings wre 4-6 coaches in winter and up to ten in summer on Saturday. In August 1934 two D49/2 'Hunt' Class engines arrived new at the shed, No. 230 'The Brocklesby' and 238 'The Burton' to be 'pinched' by the covetous eyes of Botanic in 1935 and replaced by older models, No.318 a very rough rider and No.335.

In 1939 six C6 4-4-2s arrived, Nos. 700, 742, 784, 1776, 1792 and 1794, these engines also with a run of past, glorious days on the Scottish expresses behind them. Bridlington shed perhaps felt, once more that they were being fobbed off with old has-beens and found them big, ungainly and hard to maintain. The author remembers some of the peculiar results obtained by the Hull engines put to the task of getteing the Liverpool Cen. service, which left Doncaster each day at about 10.40am., up the bank to Conisbrough and thence to Mexborough and Sheffield Vic., where the engine would come off. The gradient was 1 in 100 and usually cleared by a D49 if in tiptop condition, though in wartime there were occasions when the ten coach train would stall and have to wait for a sufficient head of steam or a pilot from Doncaster, which would run up the parallel slow line and attach itself to the front of the train engine. This was acceptable if the town pilot came along, a well kept GN 'Atlantic', but highly embarrassing if one of the goods pilots, a fussy J52 tank came to take charge of things. Towards the end of the war things must have become rather straitened at Botanic, as the express in question was hauled on occasion by a D17, which just managed the climb, and C6 which collapsed wheezing in th middle of its best efforts. It must be said that never during the war was any Great Central engine, goods or passenger, seen to fail on this particular gradient.

Also in 1939 two newcomers appeared on shed, D20s Nos. 1234 and 2016, which were of much use. In 1940s the C6s went, to be replaced by four more D20s, the shed keeping to four, even if withdrawals occurred. The D49s seem to have disappeared for a time but returned in the shape of 62701/7 to Bridlington in 1949, then 62703/50 from Botanic and 62766 from Gateshead. This regime survived until displacement by dmus in 1957.

Two small Sentinel shunters, Nos. 174 and 100 were stationed at Bridlington, one to shunt the goods yard, the other the roadside stations to Driffield each day. Two G5 0-4-4Ts were actually the last steam engines on the depot, until 1958.

There was also a time in the early sixties when some of the dmus had to be withdrawn for attention or modification, and one or two VI Class 2-6-2Ts appeared on passenger workings for a short time. Presumably these went to Brid. shed and one sunny morning a pillar of smoke and steam could be seen over Driffield station as Arthur Dove, ready for retirement, had the time of his life bringing the morning Hull flier round the curve with a full head of steam on.

The D49s. List of Names

205	The Albrighton	238	The Burton
283	The Middleton	214	The Atherstone
245	The Lincolnshire	292	The Southwold
220	The Zetland	251	Derbyshire (62701)
320	Warwickshire	298	The Pytchley (62750)
222	The Berkeley	253	Oxfordshire
318	Cambridgeshire	230	The Brocklesby
234	Yorkshire	256	Hertfordshire (62703)
269	The Cleveland	322	Huntingdonshire
282	The Hurworth	236	Lancashire (62707)
327	Nottinghamshire	335	Bedfordshire
336	The Quorn	377	The Tynedale

AIRFIELDS CLOSE TO THE LINE

(Details from 'Yorkshire Airfields in World War Two.' by P. Otter.)

Carnaby was known as a special emergency runway for aircraft unable to make it back to their own base, due to battle damage, inability to rid themselves of bomb loads or mechanical failure. Two other sites were built at Manston and Woodbridge. The site at Carnaby had been used in the First War, being only some two miles from the sea and so convenient for anti-submarine patrols, then, in peacetime retained some use for private flying. During wartime in April 1944, Monks, the contractors completed a soft landing strip 3,000yd. in length and 250yd. wide, of sea sand and bitumen wth grass overshoots at each end. This was divided into three lanes, the left for emergencies only, where no permission was required, and two others side by side where aircraft could land together if needed. Offices were minimal, apart from the usual items and a control tower. The new FIDO system of ground flares to disperse fog was tried here and brought into regular use, causing initial consternation to the near-by blacked out town of Bridlington who feared some disaster. For this a siding was put in to cater for the fuel tanks. More than 1,500 aircraft were recovered, half with mechanical failure, the biggest event happening in January 1945 when 65 US bombers were diverted here en bloc after a failed raid on Brunswick. The airfield closed in March 1946, reopening in 1953 as a relief landing ground. Later, the field became a base for Thor ballistic missiles, which were suddenly removed in 1963. In the end Bridlington UDC bought the site for an industrial estate, as today.

Lissett, near Burton Agnes, opened in 1941 as a bomber base for Halifaxes. After the War this large airfield soon reverted to agricultural use.

Hutton Cranswick opened as a No.12 Group fighter airfield in January 1942, providing much of the day-time cover for East Yorks. The airfield, now an industrial estate, was on the far side of the road and villages, with three concrete runways and two T2 type hangars. Accommodation was at a distance, in huts dispersed around Watton nearby. Squadron numbers tended to rotate at airbases, as bomber losses caused amalgamation here and there. The first Spitfire Squadron here was No. 610. Soon the base was used for 'rest and training', plus a little target towing for the AA gunners along the coast. The base closed in June 1946.

Driffield was eventually the biggest and was indeed one of the oldest RAF bases locally, the furthest east of the big bomber bases and the only one with an unpleasant tale to tell.

A B1 4•6•0 No. 61012 relaxes during shunting duty in Bridlington yard. Photo. C T Goode

61410 arr. at Bridlington on 190 ex Sheffield, Victoria. August 1955. One of the unrebuilt, and best looking B16 4•6•0s No. 61410 ambles into Bridlington with an excursion from Sheffield Victoria in August 1955. There is a wealth of detail on the signal gantry, with six upper quandrant and three lower quadrant arms. The arm in front, however, is on its own post, a few feet away from the rest. Photo. K Hoole/N Stead Collection

The site is still very evident to the west of the town at Kelleythorpe, where the by-pass begins. Like others, it began life in World War 1, with wooden buildings which were eventually disposed of. Time passed until 1932, when the site was reconsidered as one of 14 suitable in the North East for airfield construction, so that RAF Driffield opened on 30th July 1936 with five brick hangars, good accommodation and instruction blocks. At first it was home to No. 3 Group bomber squadron which flew the older Whitleys who, on 5th September 1939 made the first sortie over the Ruhr with leaflets. Rather early in the war, surprisingly, the Whitley force went to Turin on a raid, refuelling in Jersey and joining others en route. Possibly this rather feeble activity must have incensed the other side, as on 15th August 1940 a force of fifty Junker Ju 88s left its base in Denmark to bomb the airfield. Reports say that only between 12 and 40 managed to reach the target due to interception on the coast, wreaking havoc on a totally unprepared and undermanned base, with but one suitable AA gun. Thirteen died, twelve Whitleys were destroyed on the ground and most of the buildings heavily damaged, so that the airfield closed until January 1941. Eventually it reopened as a fighter base for the Canadians who moved up from Leconfield, followed by New Zealanders. In 1942 Wellingtons formed the first Canadian bomber squadron. However, the runways were still grass, which precluded the use of Halifaxes; rather too late, concrete runways came in early 1944 in time for the personnel of the new battle school, trained by the army, and the inevitable target towing. After a further short stay by a squadron of Halifaxes, the war finished and, finally, matters were handed over to the Army School of Mechanical Transport.

Leconfield was also in the early scheme of things as above, opening as a No.3 group bomber airfield in December 1936. The whole field still lies close to and is visible from the railway line at Arram. The aerodrome was deemed surplus to requirements by June 1939, but managed to send ten Whitleys as part of the leaflet raid above during September 1939. From 15th August 1940 Spitfire and Blenheim squadrons were based here, and No. 616 squadron was scrambled to Flamborough Head to try to head off the Ju 88s heading for Driffield. Seven fighters were hit and another three badly damaged; this was the first and last time that Leconfield fighters were involved in active combat.

The fighters may have been silent, but the bombers stationed here were certainly not. Well equipped with all facilites from 2nd December 1942, Leconfield became an important bomber base, firstly with an Australian squadron, No. 466 which made visits to Brest, Wilhelmshafen and Essen, while North Sea patrols went on regularly. In April 1943 No. 196 squadron was added, with raids ensuing to Mannheim, Duisburg and Wuppertal, then on the night of 29th December No. 466 squadron made a big attack on Berlin. There were pre D-Day attacks on various railways yards, and towards the end of hostilities raids on Chemnitz and Wangerooge in March 1945. Soon No. 96 squadron was formed at Leconfield within Transport Command, while 640 squadron was disbanded here in May. For the next twenty years the base became a fighter airfield housing the new names, such as Meteor, Hunter, Lightning and Javelin. In 1977 the base went to the Army School of Transport as today, though the RAF has a presence with Sea-King air-sea rescue helicopters for emergency purposes.

A return Scarborough - Leicester Saturday working leaves Bridlington headed by D49 4•4•0 No. 62775 'The Tynedale', unusually in front of the the smaller engine, a 'Standard'2•6•0.

Photo. K Hoole/N Stead Collection

During wartime, service personnel were the most privileged and most visible of railway travellers, and it is fitting that the RAF should be mentioned in connection with this railway history. Days of National Service spring to mind and possibly movements would be much the same in wartime as afterwards; servicemen and women on transfer to another posting would be issued with a paper warrant by the camp office, while going on a 36 or 48 hour weekend leave would be different in that tickets for the coming weekend would be issued at the station on pay day (Thursdays), when a railway rep. would be present at the larger locations to produce what would be required, often a blank ticket with the destination hand written. Transport, in the shape of a lorry or even a bus would run to the nearest railhead, perhaps Bridlington, Beverley or Driffield, which were big enough to cope with increased traffic at weekends. Returning personnel might well leave the train at a station nearer to the base - the one most likely filling the bill here would be Carnaby which was virtually on the doorstep. Arram was close, but at some distance from living quarters.

Carnaby's collected ticket lists survive, beginning in 1926 at 151 for the month of June and rising and falling a little to 256 in July 1930 and with the trend to be below 100 per month to April 1934 when numbers went above 100 once more. In August there was usually a surge, to 306 at this time, probably a village outing or school day out. This surge was to 332 in August 1937, in the midst of other months only registering the mid hundreds. Prior to 1939 numbers were low, at 60 or 70, and indeed remained low until April 1943 after which two columns are shown in the collected tickets, for workmen's and standard returns etc., as shown:-

1943

Weekend totals.	Workmen's.	Ordinaries.
(for month)		
July 3rd	1376	
July 10th	2530	
July 17th	2184	405
July 24th	1655	
July 31st	4087	
Oct 30th	5307	243
Dec 11th	3600	
Dec 18th	2633	229
Dec 24th	2956	
Dec 31st	5816	

During Jan. to June in 1944 the four figure totals continued, until reducing from 1662 to 106 workmen's in the second half-year. All subsequent tickets collected are shown by taking the month of August as an example thereafter:

1945: 436.	1946: 398.	1947: 464.	1948: 341.
1949: 152.	1950: 174.	1951: 223	1952: 93.
1953: 126.	1959: 173.	1961: 76.	1963: 25
1965: 27.	1967: 28.	1969: 26.	

The station closed 3rd January 1970.

THE LOCKINGTON ACCIDENT

On a fine and sunny day, Saturday 27th July 1986, the 09.33 stopping train for Hull left Bridlington with a fair load of returning holidaymakers. The service consisted of two twin dmus. setting out on the 31 mile, 49 minute run which the driver had covered many times before, a quiet line without much to disturb it. At 09.55 the train halted at Hutton Cranswick and then set off to pass the long closed station at Lockington, some three miles south. Here was an OAC, a crossing without barriers but with flashing lights monitored remotely. Unfortunately, a Ford Escort van driver decided to take a chance with his vehicle and began to cross in front of the train which was appearing round the curve at some 70mph. The train struck the van squarely and smashed it to pieces, while the train ran on for 150yd. before derailing completely, the first coach slewing round on itself, the remaining three coaches lying haphazard over both lines. Passengers had been thrown through the windows, there being eight dead and 32 injuries. A boy of eleven in the van was killed; one assumes its driver had been flung clear.

This was the worst accident of its kind on British Railways since the Hixon collision between a Manchester to Euston express and a heavy road vehicle, though half barriers were installed in the latter case. Lockington was one of only 39 other AOCs in this country.

Track Layouts

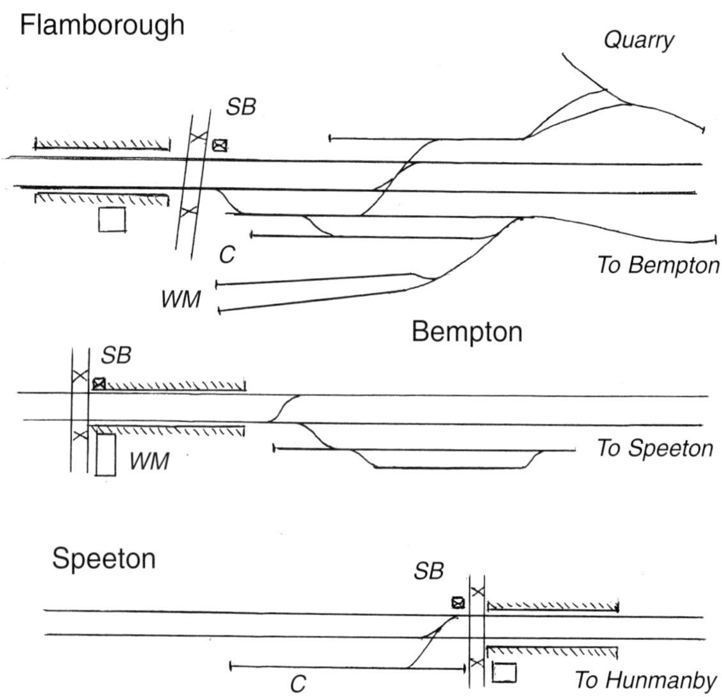

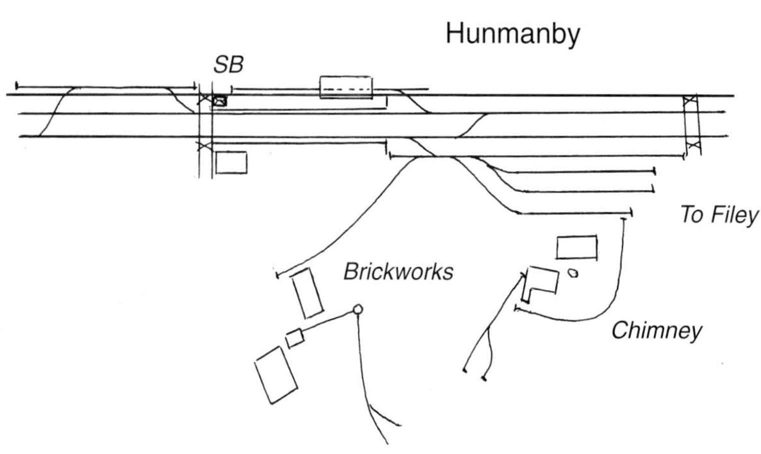

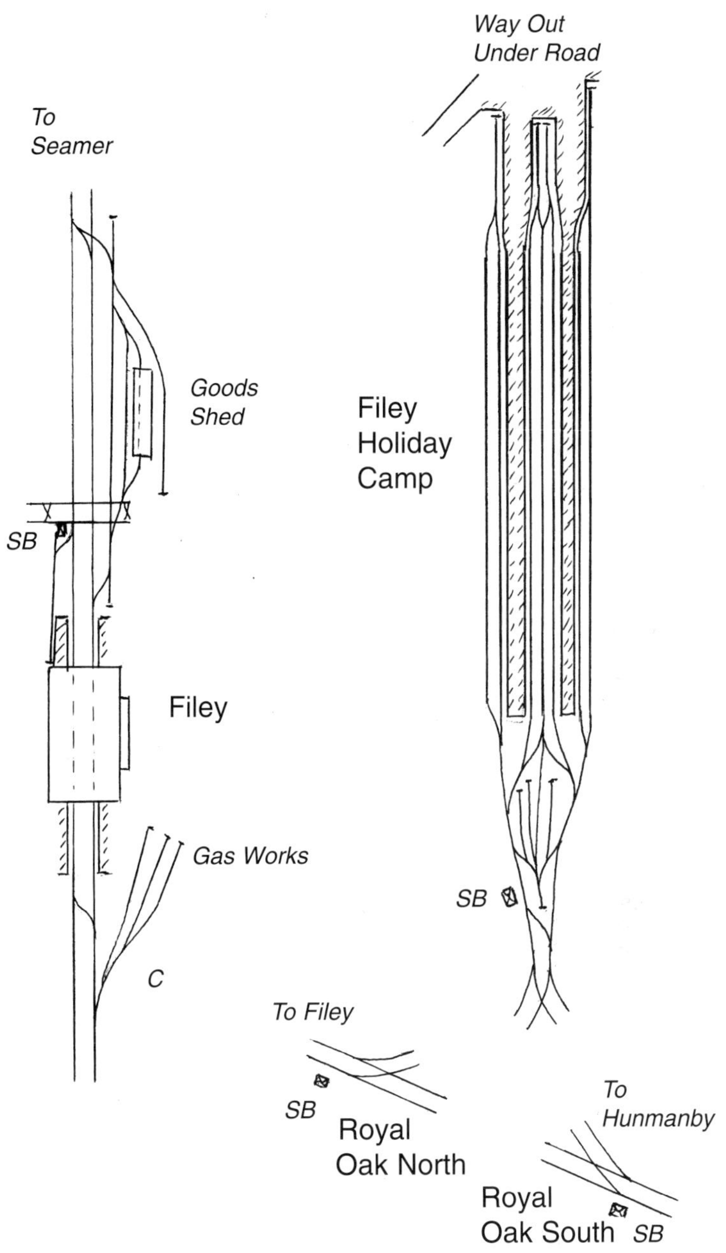
Way Out
Under Road
To
Seamer
Goods
Shed
Filey
Holiday
Camp
SB
Filey
Gas Works
SB
C
To Filey
SB
Royal
Oak North
To
Hunmanby
Royal
Oak South
SB

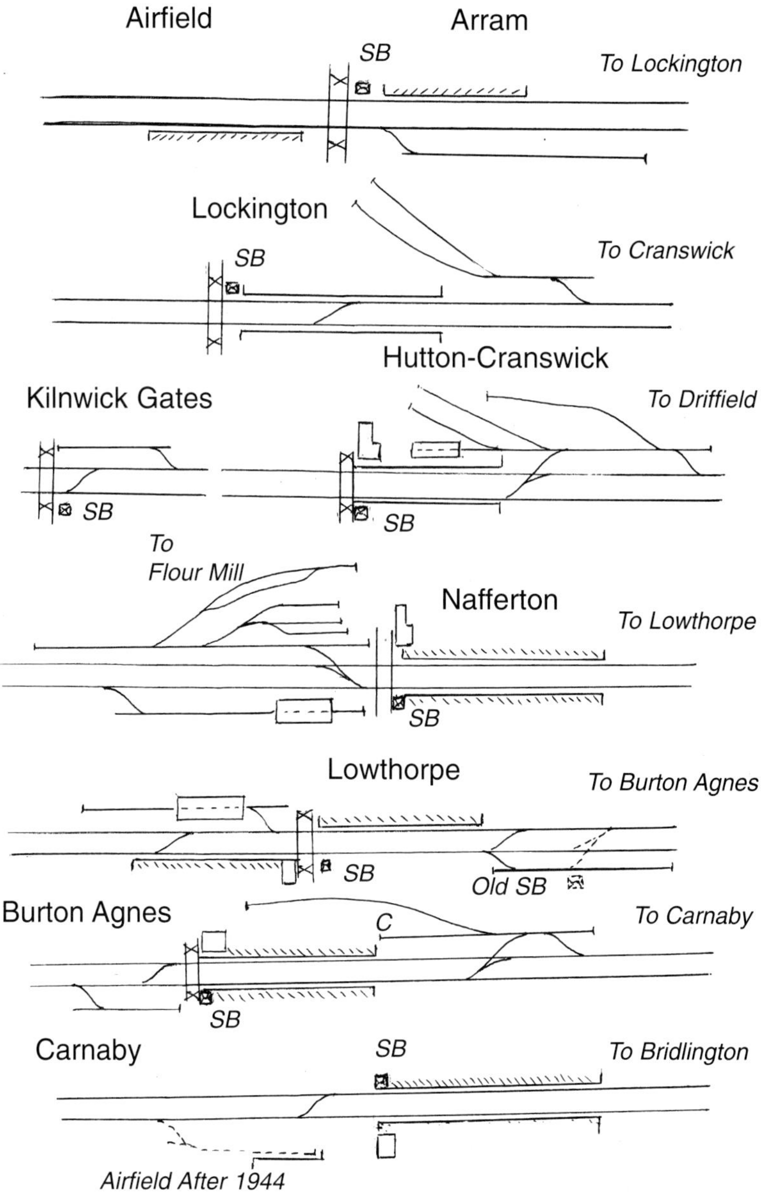
Airfield
Arram
SB
To Lockington
Lockington
SB
To Cranswick
Hutton-Cranswick
Kilnwick Gates
To Driffield
SB
SB
To
Flour Mill
Nafferton
To Lowthorpe
SB
Lowthorpe
To Burton Agnes
SB
Old SB
Burton Agnes
C
To Carnaby
SB
Carnaby
SB
To Bridlington
Airfield After 1944

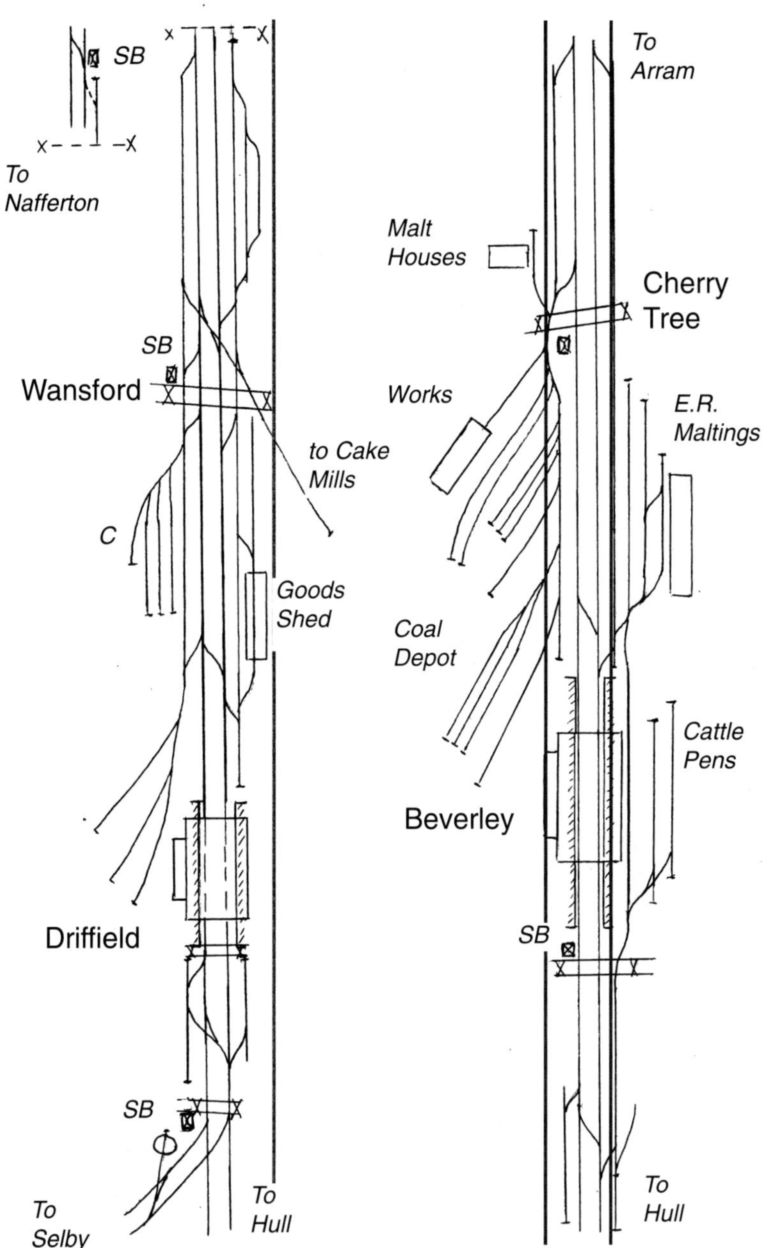
SB
To
Nafferton
SB
Wansford
to Cake
Mills
C
Goods
Shed
Driffield
SB
To
Selby
To
Hull
To
Arram
Malt
Houses
Cherry
Tree
Works
E.R.
Maltings
Coal
Depot
Cattle
Pens
Beverley
SB
To
Hull

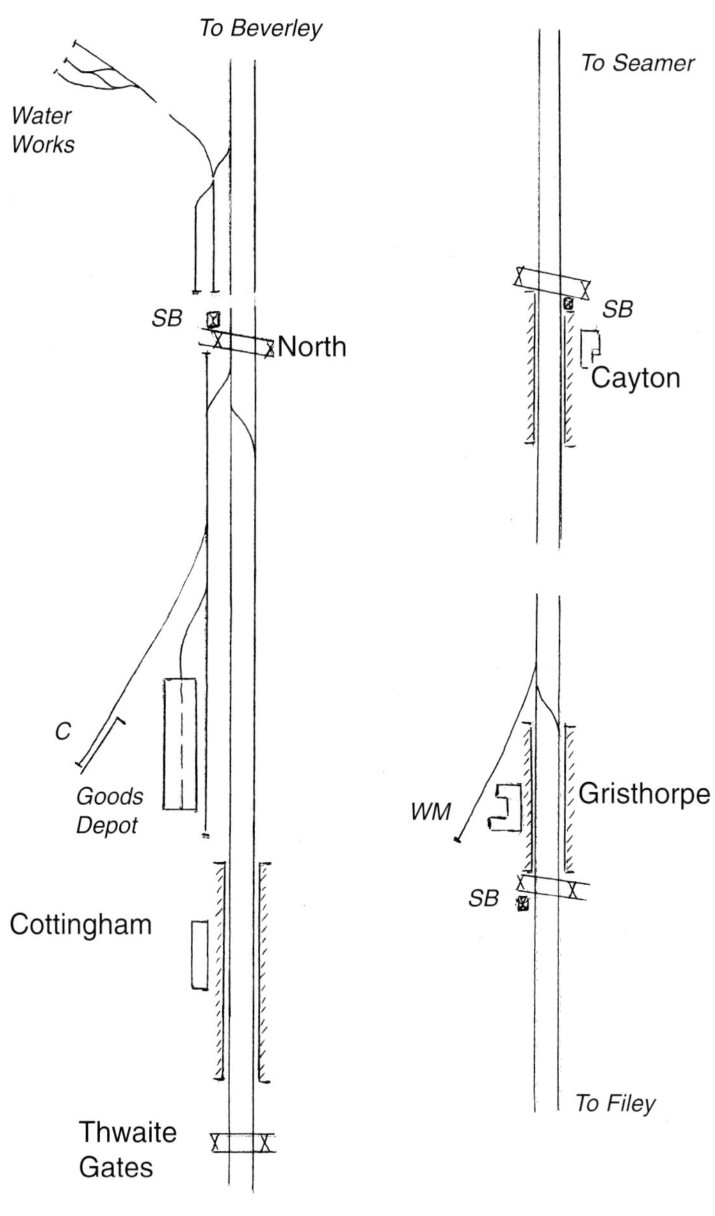
To Beverley
Water
Works
SB
North
C
Goods
Depot
Cottingham
Thwaite
Gates
To Seamer
SB
Cayton
Gristhorpe
WM
SB
To Filey

c 1928

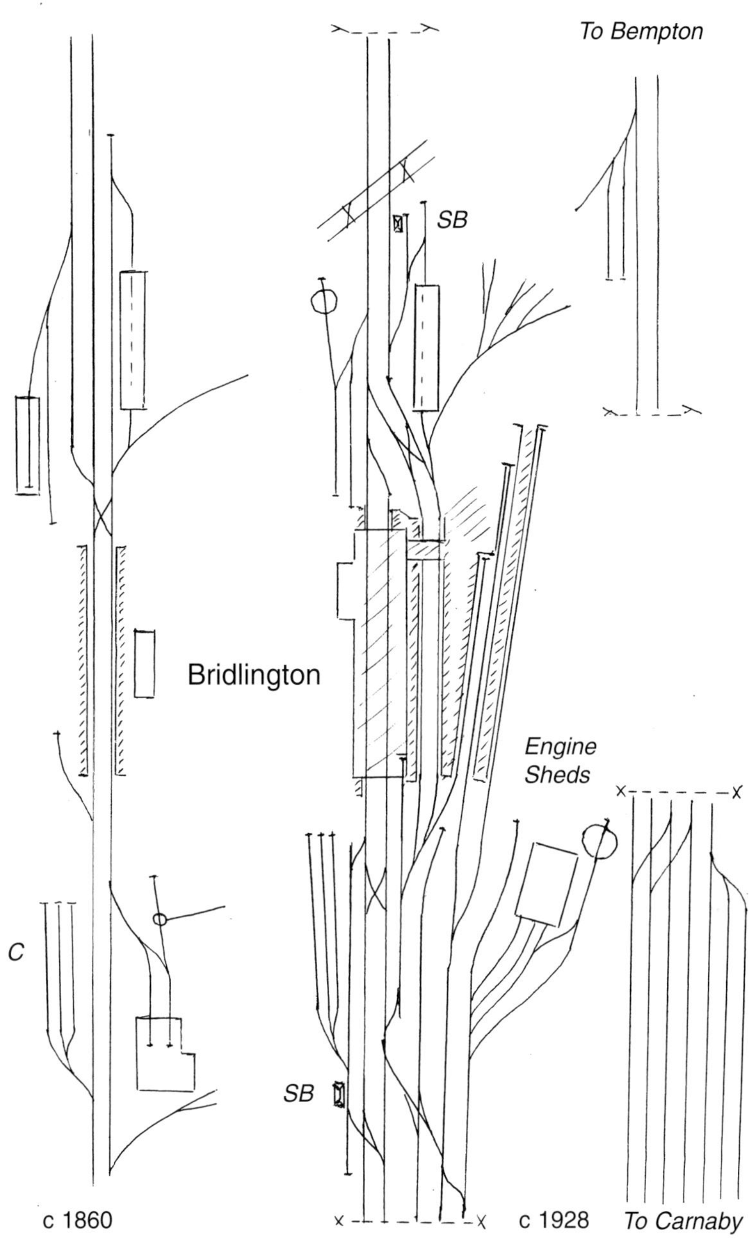
To Bempton
SB
Bridlington
Engine
Sheds
C
SB
c 1860
c 1928
To Carnaby

BRITISH RAILWAYS

Revised fares from 20/10/58

CHEAP SINGLE
AND RETURN
DAY TICKETS
ANY TRAIN — ANY DAY

	FROM											
	Bempton		Filey		Flam-borough		Gris-thorpe		Hun-manby		Speeton	
	Sngle s d	Rtn s d	Sngle s d	Rtn s d	Sngle s d	Rtn s d	Sngle s d	Rtn s d	Sngle s d	Rtn s d	Sngle s d	Rtn s d
Arram	3/2	5/7	3/11	7/6	2/11	5/1	4/2	7/7	3/8	6/9	3/5	6/–
Bempton	—	—	1/–	1/11	–/3	–/4	1/2	2/3	–/10	1/7	–/5	–/9
Beverley	3/8	6/–	4/3	7/6	3/6	5/9	4/7	7/10	4/2	7/4	3/11	6/8
Bridlington	–/8	–/11	1/5	2/10	–/6	–/9	1/7	3/2	1/2	2/4	–/10	1/8
Burton Agnes	1/3	2/–	2/4	4/3	1/1	1/9	2/6	4/5	2/–	3/7	1/7	2/8
Carnaby	1/–	1/5	2/–	3/6	–/10	1/2	2/3	3/8	1/9	2/11	1/4	2/1
Cloughton	—	4/8	—	3/4	—	5/1	—	2/10	—	4/–	—	4/6
Cottingham	4/–	6/6	4/7	8/–	3/10	6/6	4/10	8/2	4/5	7/10	4/2	7/3
Driffield	2/1	3/6	3/1	5/6	2/–	3/3	3/3	5/8	2/9	4/11	2/3	4/–
Filey	1/–	1/11	—	—	1/3	2/5	–/4	–/7	–/5	–/9	–/11	1/8
Flamborough	–/3	–/4	1/3	2/5	—	—	1/5	2/9	1/–	2/–	–/7	1/2
Fyling Hall	—	6/3	—	4/11	—	6/8	—	4/7	—	5/7	—	6/1
Gristhorpe	1/2	2/3	–/4	–/7	1/5	2/9	—	—	–/8	1/2	1/1	2/–
Hawsker	—	7/2	—	5/10	—	7/7	—	5/4	—	6/6	—	7/–
Hayburn Wyke	—	5/2	—	3/10	—	5/7	—	3/4	—	4/6	—	5/–
Hull	4/4	7/6	5/–	9/–	4/2	7/3	5/2	9/3	4/11	8/9	4/6	8/–
Hunmanby	–/10	1/7	–/5	–/9	1/–	2/–	–/8	1/2	—	—	–/9	1/2
Hutton Cranswick ...	2/3	4/3	3/3	6/2	2/1	4/0	3/5	6/4	3/–	5/9	2/6	4/11
Lockington	2/10	4/11	3/9	7/–	2/7	4/6	3/11	7/3	3/6	6/5	3/1	5/6
Lowthorpe	1/6	2/6	2/6	4/8	1/4	2/3	2/9	4/9	2/4	4/–	1/10	3/2
Market Weighton ...	—	—	—	8/6	—	—	—	—	—	—	—	—
Nafferton	1/8	2/11	2/8	5/2	1/6	2/8	2/11	5/2	2/6	4/6	2/–	3/6
Pocklington	—	—	—	8/6	—	—	—	—	—	—	—	—
Ravenscar	—	5/8	—	4/4	—	6/1	—	3/10	—	5/–	—	5/6
Robin Hoods Bay ...	—	6/7	—	5/5	—	7/–	—	5/1	—	6/1	—	6/5
Scarborough	1/8	3/4	1/–	2/–	1/11	3/9	–/9	1/6	1/4	2/8	1/7	3/2
Seamer	1/7	3/1	–/11	1/8	1/10	3/7	–/8	1/2	1/3	2/3	1/6	2/11
Speeton	–/5	–/9	–/11	1/8	–/7	1/2	1/1	2/–	–/9	1/2	—	—
Staintondale	—	5/2	—	3/10	—	5/7	—	3/4	—	4/6	—	5/–
Whitby Town	—	8/–	—	6/8	—	8/5	—	6/2	—	7/4	—	7/10
Whitby West Cliff ...	—	8/–	—	6/8	—	8/5	—	6/2	—	7/4	—	7/10
York	—	8/6	—	8/6	—	8/6	—	8/3	—	8/6	—	8/6

ALSO AVAILABLE IN REVERSE DIRECTION

FIRST CLASS 50% ABOVE SECOND CLASS FARES

Tickets obtainable at stations and rail ticket agencies

NOTICE AS TO CONDITIONS

These tickets are issued subject to the Regulations and Conditions in the Commission's Publications and Notices applicable to British Railways. Luggage allowances are as set out in the Conditions.

No. 41

Published by British Railways (N.E. Region) 10/58 Printed in Great Britain ERO 39694/1 (R19267) Herald, York—C2

BRITISH RAILWAYS

Q 698 (HD)x

ATTRACTIONS AT HULL

Jameson Street, Illuminations 26th November to 24th December

FOOTBALL AT HULL

ASSOCIATION

Sat. 29th Nov. v. Queens Pk. Rangers

Sat. 13th Dec. v. Doncaster Rovers

RUGBY LEAGUE

Sat. 29th Nov. Hull v. Leigh

Sat. 6th Dec. Hull v. Featherstone R.

Sat. 13th Dec. Hull K.R. v. Hunslet

Sat. 20th Dec. Hull v. Wakefield Trinity

Excursion Bookings to

HULL

For CHRISTMAS SHOPPING

By any ordinary train from 11-0 a.m., returning same day by ordinary train (except 5-30 p.m. from Hull)

EACH WEEKDAY

Wednesday 26th November to Wednesday 24th December

Convenient Outward Services						SX		Second Class Return Fares
		a.m.	a.m.	p.m.	p.m.	p.m.	p.m.	s d
Scarborough	dep	—	11 30	1 10	—	—	—	8 6
Seamer	,,	—	11 37	1 16	—	—	—	8 0
Filey	,,	—	11 50	1 28	—	—	—	7 6
Hunmanby	,,	—	11 55	1 33	—	—	—	7 0
Speeton	,,	—	—	1 41	—	—	—	6 6
			p.m.					
Bempton	,,	—	12 5	1 46	—	—	—	6 6
Flamborough	,,	—	12 8	1 49	—	—	—	6 0
Bridlington	,,	11 0	12 14	1 55	3 36	4 32	5 26	5 6
Carnaby	,,	—	—	1 59	—	4 36	5 31	4 9
Burton Agnes ..	,,	—	12 21	—	3 45	4 41	5 36	4 6
Lowthorpe	,,	—	12 25	2 6	3 49	4 45	5 40	4 6
Nafferton	,,	—	12 30	2 11	3 54	4 50	5 45	3 9
Driffield	,,	11 16	12 36	2 17	4 0	4 56	5 52	3 6
Hutton Cranswick	,,	—	12 41	2 22	4 7	5 1	5 57	3 3
Lockington	,,	—	12 47	2 28	4 13	—	6 3	2*11
Arram	,,	—	12 51	2 32	4 18	5 9	6 7	2* 8
Beverley	,,	11 30	1 0	2 40	4 26	5 18	6 16	2* 0
Cottingham	,,	11 36	1 6	2 46	4 33	5 24	6 22	1* 0
Hull	arr	11 43	1 13	2 53	4 41	5 31	6 29	—

SX—Saturdays excepted.
*—Cheap Day Return Fare available by any train on day of issue.

RETURN SERVICES

HULL depart		
3 45 p.m.	for	Cottingham, Beverley, Arram, Driffield, Nafferton, Bridlington and intermediate stations to Scarborough (except Seamer).
4 35 p.m.	for	all intermediate stations to Bridlington.
5 10 p.m. SX	for	Beverley, Driffield, Bridlington, Filey and Scarborough.
5 45 p.m.	for	all intermediate stations to Scarborough.
6 45 p.m.	for	Cottingham, Beverley, Driffield and Bridlington.
8 15 p.m.	for	all intermediate stations to Bridlington.
9 45 p.m.	for	all intermediate stations to Bridlington (except Carnaby).

SX—Saturdays excepted.

Children under three years of age, free ; three years and under fourteen, half-fares.

Further information will be supplied on application to the Stations, or to the District Traffic Superintendent, Carmichael Chambers, George Street, Hull, Tel. 31739 (Extn. 48). and District Traffic Superintendent York, Tel. 53022 (Ext. 397.)

NOTICE AS TO CONDITIONS

These tickets are issued subject to the Regulations and Conditions in the Commission's Publications and Notices applicable to British Railways. Luggage Allowances are as set out in the conditions.

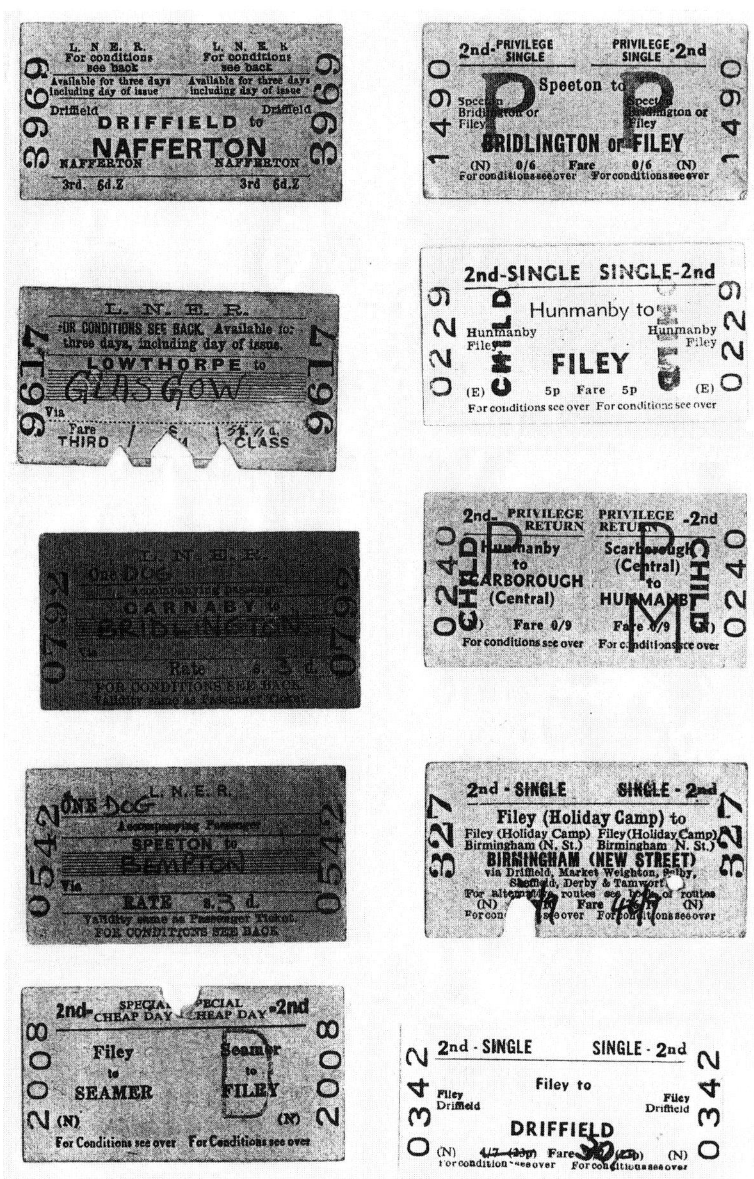

Collection of tickets from Chris Goode

2nd-SINGLE SINGLE-2nd
0075
Hunmanby to
Hunmanby Hunmanby
Hull (Paragon) Hull (Paragon)
HULL (PARAGON)
CHILD
(E) 21p Fare 21p (E)
For conditions see over For conditions see over

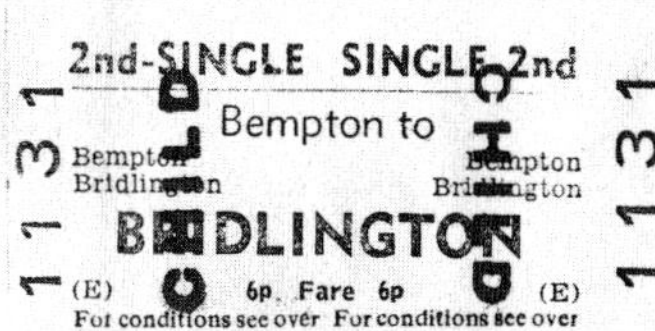

2nd-SINGLE SINGLE-2nd
1131
Bempton to
Bempton Bempton
Bridlington Bridlington
BRIDLINGTON
CHILD
(E) 6p Fare 6p (E)
For conditions see over For conditions see over

2nd-PRIVILEGE RETURN PRIVILEGE RETURN-2nd
5138
Driffield or Lowthorpe to NAFFERTON
Nafferton to DRIFFIELD or LOWTHORPE
(N) Fare 0/5 Fare 0/5 (N)
For conditions see over For conditions see over

2nd-SINGLE SINGLE-2nd
0512
Hutton Cranswick to
Hutton Cranswick Hutton Cranswick
Cottingham Cottingham
COTTINGHAM
(E) 21p Fare 23P (E)
For conditions see over For conditions see over

2nd-SINGLE SINGLE-2nd
3750
Driffield to
Driffield Driffield
Nafferton Nafferton
NAFFERTON
(E) 6p Fare 6p (E)
For conditions see over For conditions see over

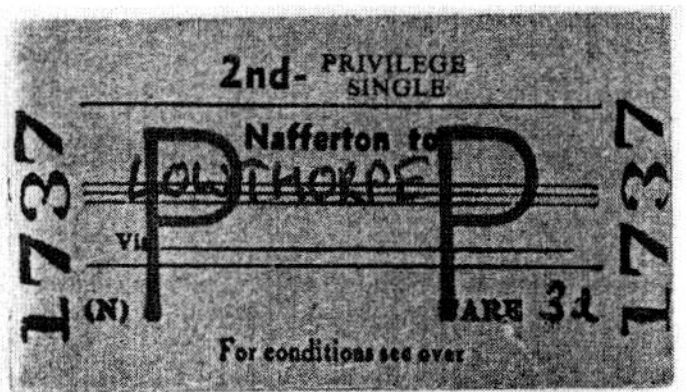

2nd- PRIVILEGE SINGLE
1737
Nafferton to
LOWTHORPE
(N) FARE 3d
For conditions see over

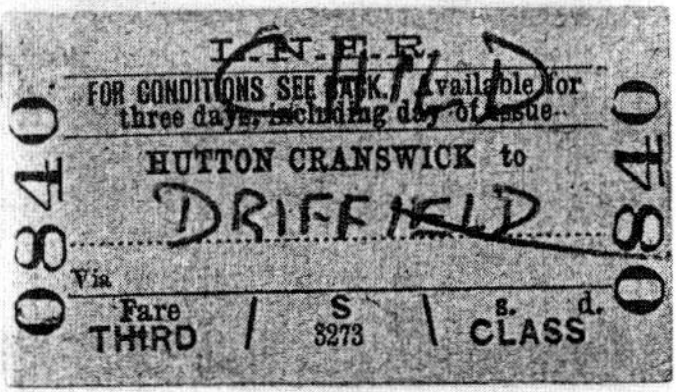

L.N.E.R.
CHILD
FOR CONDITIONS SEE BACK. Available for three days, including day of issue.
0840
HUTTON CRANSWICK to
DRIFFIELD
Via
Fare THIRD S 3273 s. d. CLASS

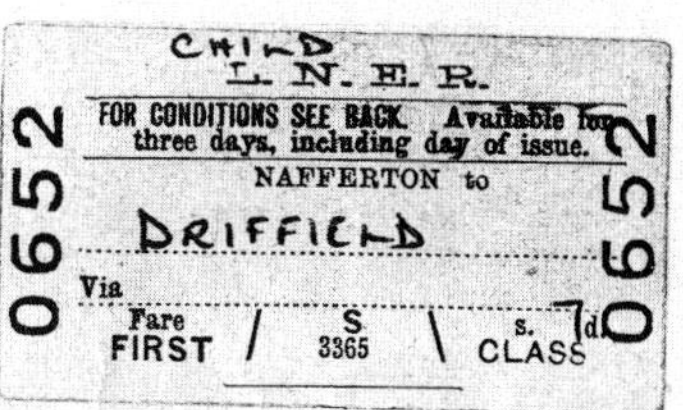

CHILD
L. N. E. R.
FOR CONDITIONS SEE BACK. Available for three days, including day of issue.
0652
NAFFERTON to
DRIFFIELD
Via
Fare FIRST S 3365 s. 7d. CLASS

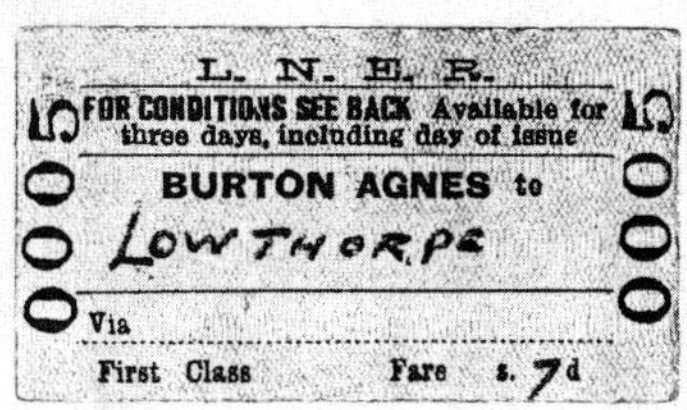

L. N. E. R.
FOR CONDITIONS SEE BACK Available for three days, including day of issue
0005
BURTON AGNES to
LOWTHORPE
Via
First Class Fare s. 7d

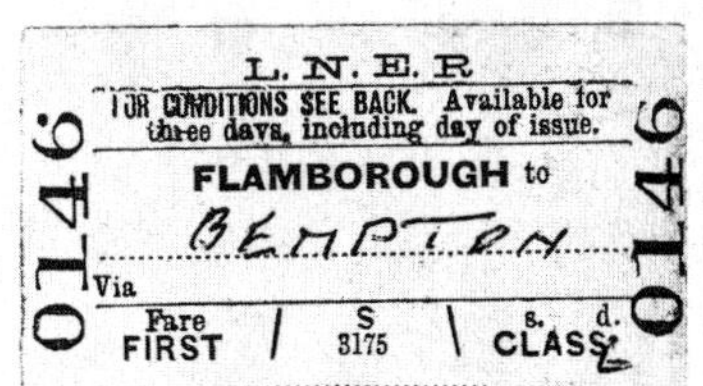

L. N. E. R
FOR CONDITIONS SEE BACK. Available for three days, including day of issue.
0146
FLAMBOROUGH to
BEMPTON
Via
Fare FIRST S 3175 s. d. CLASS

LIST OF OTHER PUBLICATIONS BY THE AUTHOR

'The York & Scarborough Railway'.
'The Birmingham & Gloucester Loop'.
'The Mexborough & Swinton Traction Company'.*
'The Burton & Ashby Light Railway'.
'Railways of South Yorkshire'.*
'Railways of North Lincs'.
'The Wakefield, Pontefract & Goole Railway'.
'The Railways of Castleford'.
'Huddersfield Branch Lines'.
'The Railways of Hull'.*
'The Selby & Driffield Railway'.
'To the Crystal Palace', (Forge Books)
'To the Alexandra Palace'. (Forge Books)
'Trentham, the Gardens and Branch Railway'.
'Doncaster's Trams & Trolleybuses'.
'The Dearne District Light Railways'.
'The Selby & Goole Railway'. (Oakwood)*
'The Wensleydale Branch'. (Oakwood)*
'The Hertford Loop'. (Oakwood)*
'Railways of East Yorkshire'. (Oakwood)*

(denotes those that are out of print but which may be in stock or available in libraries).*